Trade in the Asian Pacific Region

Trade in the Asian Pacific Region

Edited by
A.M. Babkina

Nova Science Publishers
New York

Art Director: Maria Ester Hawrys
Assistant Director: Elenor Kallberg
Graphics: Denise Dieterich, Kerri Pfister,
Erika Cassutti and Barbara Minerd
Manuscript Coordinator: Sharyn Beers Schweidel
Book Production: Tammy Sauter, Gavin Aghamore
Christine Mathosian and Joanne Bennette
Circulation: Irene Kwartiroff and Annette Hellinger

Library of Congress Cataloging-in-Publication Data available upon request

ISBN 1-56072-358-0

6080 Jericho Turnpike, Suite 207
Commack, New York 11725
Tele. 516-499-3103 Fax 516-499-3146
E Mail Novascil@aol.com

Printed in the United States of America

Contents

U.S. Trade and Market Access Problems with Asia: An Overview

APEC AND FREE TRADE IN THE ASIA PACIFIC*

Dick K. Nanto

SUMMARY

The Asia Pacific Economic Cooperation (APEC) forum is an organization of eighteen economies surrounding the Pacific Ocean that promotes open trade and closer economic cooperation in the Asia/Pacific region. Its membership includes the United States, Canada, Mexico, and Chile in the Americas, Japan, South Korea, China, Taiwan, and Hong Kong in East Asia, the ASEAN nations of Indonesia, Brunei, Malaysia, Singapore, Thailand, and The Philippines, plus the Oceanic nations of Australia, New Zealand, and Papua New Guinea.

APEC is of interest to the Congress because it is committed to dismantling all barriers to trade and investment among its members by the year 2010 for industrialized member economies or 2020 for the remainder. This future free-trade area would cover nearly half the world's population, 60 percent of the world's gross domestic product, and 40 percent of world trade. APEC may define the framework for America's future trading relationships with the fast-growing Asian region. If APEC achieves its goals, the United States would establish free trade with nations, such as Japan and China, that are responsible for about half of the U.S. trade deficit and which account for many of the U.S. trade problems. Since trade barriers in Asia are higher than those in the United States, however, the United States seems to have more to gain in the process than it loses. Free trade among Asian nations, moreover, may allow more Asian exports to be absorbed at home rather than being directed at the U.S. market.

On November 19, 1995, the leaders of APEC met in Osaka, Japan, where they agreed to an action Agenda that is intended to translate the vision of an APEC free-trade area into reality. This Action Agenda is the template for future APEC work to accomplish the three common goals of (1) trade and investment liberali-

---

* Excerpted from *CRS Report* 95-1079

zation, (2) trade and investment facilitation, and (3) economic and technical co-operation. The Agenda laid out nine general principles which are to guide individual APEC members in devising national Action Plans (to be submitted in 1996) to attain the goal. The Action Plans are to be implemented starting in January 1997. A question is whether, and at what point in the APEC process, fast-trace authority would be necessary.

There was considerable disagreement among APEC members over whether the principle of comprehensiveness in removing barriers to trade would apply to all products and commodities. Japan, China, South Korea, and Taiwan succeeded in inserting a principle of flexibility which arguably means that members would have some flexibility in liberalizing trade in sensitive sectors, such as agriculture. China also tried to obtain a definition of non-discrimination that would assure it of most-favored-nation treatment by the United States.

It terms of political feasibility, a key question remains to be answered. Would the public support a free trade area encompassing all major Asian and Pacific economies? How would the American people respond to a free-trade area that included China, Japan, and south Korea? Import-sensitive industries, such as textiles and apparel, also would likely oppose free imports from Asia.

INTRODUCTION

Asia Pacific Economic Cooperation (APEC) is an organization of eighteen economies surrounding the Pacific Ocean. along with the World Trade Organization, it is the preeminent forum for promoting open trade and closer economic cooperation in the Asia/Pacific region. Its membership includes the United States, Canada, Mexico, and Chile in the Americas, Japan, South Korea, China, Taiwan, and Hong Kong in East Asia, the ASEAN nations of Indonesia, Brunei, Malaysia, Singapore, Thailand, and The Philippines, plus the Oceanic nations of Australia, New Zealand, and Papua New Guinea.

APEC is of interest to the Congress because it is committed to dismantling all barriers to trade and investment among its members by the year 2010 or 2020. This future free-trade area would cover nearly half the world's population, 60 percent of the world's gross domestic product, and 40 percent of world trade. APEC may define the framework for America's future trading relationships with the fast-growing Asian Region. It also may provide trade and investment liberalization that goes beyond that available under the World Trade Organization. The APEC goal for liberalized trade and investment implies that free trade would be established with nations, such as Japan and China, with whom the United States runs large trade deficits and which account for many of the U.S. trade problems. (See figure 1.) Import barriers between economies such as China and Taiwan or South Korea and Japan that have diverted exports to the United States also would have to be eliminated. APEC's 1995 Action Agenda commits the United States to devising a U.S. Action Plan that would lead to free trade with other APEC members by 2010 (with implementation beginning in 1997).

The Clinton Administration has supported the APEC process and has viewed it as an institution that can bridge relationships with the Asia/Pacific in a manner similar to the post-war trans-Atlantic institutions bridged relationships with Europe. The Administration has stated that APEC is an important part of its Asia policy and represents a disciplined partnership for growth and opportunity that can create jobs, raise incomes, and give hope to people all across the Pacific.[1] In November 1995, however, Senate Republican Leader Bob Dole, called for a "cooling off period" while current trade pacts are assessed before embarking on new ones with Asia and Latin America. In discussing the Administration's request for new fast-track trade negotiating authority, Senator Dole asked why the Administration seemed to be in a hurry to pile on many more trade agreements as soon as possible from Latin America to Asia to Europe.[2]

FIGURE 1. U.S. Merchandise Trade Balances with Selected Countries, 1994

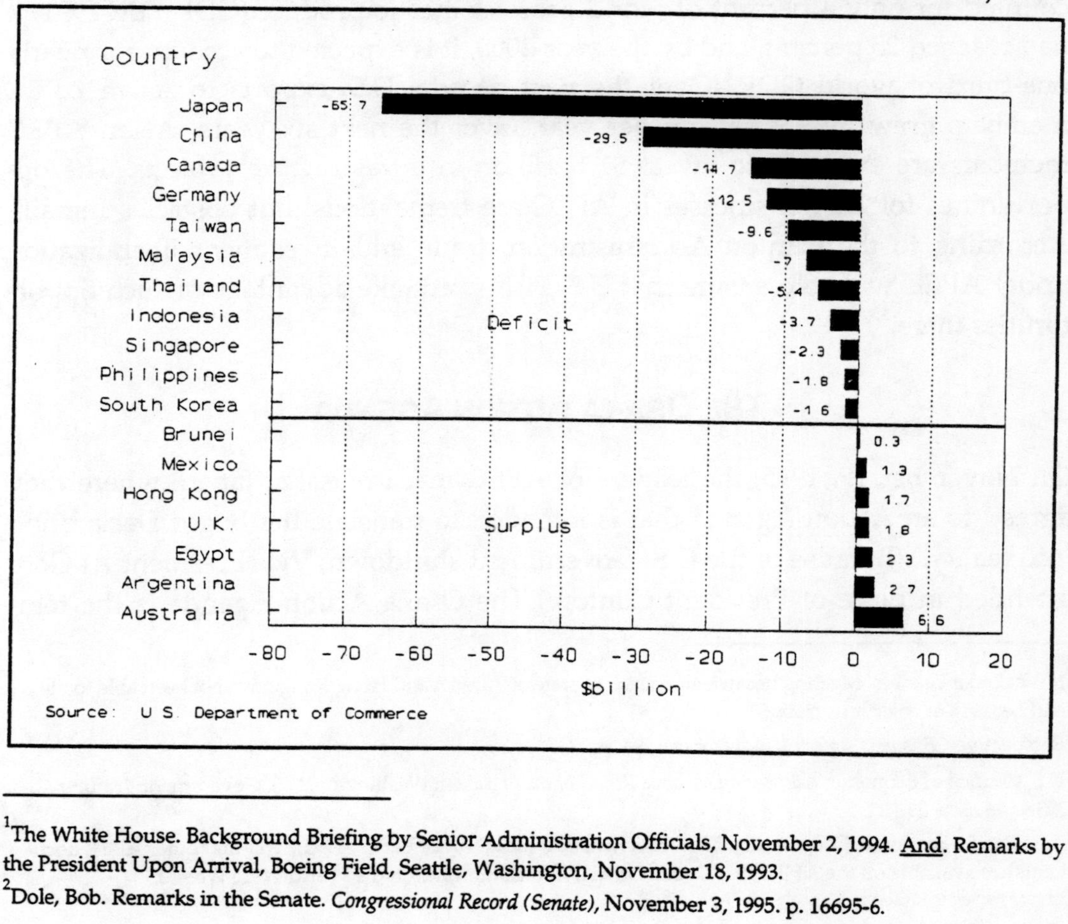

[1]The White House. Background Briefing by Senior Administration Officials, November 2, 1994. <u>And</u>. Remarks by the President Upon Arrival, Boeing Field, Seattle, Washington, November 18, 1993.

[2]Dole, Bob. Remarks in the Senate. *Congressional Record (Senate)*, November 3, 1995. p. 16695-6.

Fast-track authority for considering new trade agreements has yet to be granted to the Clinton Administration to negotiate the APEC free-trade area. A question is whether, and at what point in the APEC process, fast-track authority would be necessary.

APEC was established in 1989 at the initiative of Australia. After six years, it is evolving from a "talk shop" into a force for trade liberalization. In 1993, the United States raised APEC's profile by inviting its leaders to attend a summit[3] in Seattle. This focused world attention on the fledgling organization. At its 1994 summit in Bogor, Indonesia, APEC leaders signed a declaration setting the goal of free and open trade and investment in APEC. The industrialized economies (United States, Japan, Canada, Australia, New Zealand, Singapore, and possibly others) are to achieve the goal by the year 2010 and the remaining economies to do so by 2020. The United States argues against allowing the additional 10 years for developing economies, but it was retained primarily at the insistence of China, South Korea, and Malaysia. The Bogor Declaration is a consensus, not legal, document.

The Asia/Pacific in one of the most vibrant economic areas in the world. U.S. trade with the Pacific has surpassed that with Europe. In 1960, East Asia accounted for only 4 percent of world gross domestic product (GDP). By 1991, it had reached 25 percent, and by the year 2000, it is expected to account for nearly one-third of world GDP.[4] Over the past decade, U.S. exports to Asian APEC members grew by 9.9 percent per year. Over the next six years, Asian APEC members are expected to invest $1.1 trillion in infrastructure projects. The opportunities for U.S. businesses in APEC are tremendous, but obstacles remain. According to the Clinton Administration, trade and investment liberalization under APEC will help ensure that U.S. Firms can take advantage of such opportunities there.[5]

THE OSAKA ACTION AGENDA

On November 19, 1995, the leaders of APEC met in Osaka, Japan, where they agreed to an Action Agenda that is intended to translate the Bogor Declaration into reality.[6] (Because of the U.S. Government shutdown, Vice President Al Gore attended in place of President Clinton.) The Osaka Action Agenda is the tem-

[3] It is called a Leaders' Meeting because the heads of state of Taiwan and Hong Kong have not been able to attend because of objections from China.

[4] Perspectives. *Business America*, November 1994. pp. 4-5.

[5] U.S. Council of Economic Advisers. *Economic Report of the President*. Washington, U.S. Government Printing Office, 1995. p. 230-31.

[6] Asia Pacific Economic Cooperation. *The Osaka Action Agenda* (November 19, 1995). This and other APEC documents are available on the APEC 1995 Osaka Official Information site on the World Wide Web (http://apec.tokio.co.jp).

plate for future APEC work to accomplish the three common goals of (1) trade and investment liberalization, (2) trade and investment facilitation, and (3) economic and technical cooperation. The Agenda laid out nine general principles for members to follow in devising a road map to reach APEC's free-trade goal. These general principles are to guide individual APEC members in devising national Action Plans (to be submitted in 1996) to attain the goal. The Action Plans are to be implemented starting in January 1997.

The **general principles** in the Action Plan included (1) comprehensiveness (all impediments are to be included), (2) WTO-consistency (consistent with the World Trade Organization), (3) comparability (equal sacrifice by all), (4) non-discrimination (benefits to be accorded to all APEC members and also to non-APEC countries on a reciprocal basis), (5) transparency, (6) standstill (no new barriers), (7) simultaneous start-continuous process-differentiated time tables (all start together in a continuous process to achieve long-term goal), (8) flexibility (a controversial principle that some argue allows for sensitive sectors, such as agriculture in Japan, China, and South Korea, to be liberalized more slowly), and (9) cooperation (to pursue economic and technical cooperation).

The Agenda also outlined actions that APEC economies were to take in fifteen specific areas. These included both actions by individual members and collectively by APEC in areas such as tariffs, non-tariff measures, services, investment, standards, customs procedures, intellectual property rights (IPRs), competition policy, and dispute mediation. Under IPRs, for example, the actions included ensuring the IPRs are granted expeditiously and that adequate and effective procedures and remedies are available against infringement of IPRs.

Under **dispute mediation**, the Action Plan called for more transparency of government laws, regulations, and administrative procedures with a view toward reducing and avoiding disputes regarding trade and investment matters. APEC hopes to promote dialogue and increased understanding, including exchange of views on any matter that may lead to a dispute, and cooperatively examine on a voluntary basis disputes that arise. It also is to examine possible future evolution of procedures for the resolution of disputes. The idea is that a voluntary mechanism would be established that would rely primarily on "Asian-style mediation" to address problems not covered by the WTO (such as antitrust policy) and which would provide a multilateral forum to resolve bilateral disputes.

Each APEC member also announced **initial actions** for liberalization and facilitation of trade and investment. (See appendix A.) These actions represented the first wide-ranging initiatives of APEC members to speed up implementing their Uruguay Round commitments. For the United States, the actions did not include any acceleration of tariff reductions. The United States merely indicated which of the Uruguay Round Agreements had been implemented and which were to be implemented in 1996. It also listed other liberalization and facilitation measures taken in 1995. Japan accelerated tariff reductions on 697 items by two years, reduced tariffs on 57 agricultural and fishery products, and announced numerous deregulatory measures.

The surprise package of initial actions came from China. China indicated that it would slash substantially the tariffs on over 4,000 items to bring its average tariff rate to less than 30 percent. It also eliminated import quotas and other import control measures on 170 items that account for about 30 percent of all such controls. This large package of measures was viewed by many as part of the attempt by China to meet the conditions for membership in the World Trade Organization.

Under **economic and technical cooperation**, the Action Agenda included compiling and sharing of data and information, surveys, training, seminars, research and technical demonstrations, and policy dialogues. Areas of cooperation included human resources development, industrial science and technology, small enterprises, energy, transportation, telecommunications, tourism, trade and investment data, trade promotion, marine resources conservation, fisheries, and agricultural technology.

Since Japan hosted the 1995 APEC meetings, it held the Chair and the responsibility to insure that the APEC process continued. Japan, however, took this opportunity to lead a group (including South Korea, China, and Taiwan) of members who argued for a weak definition of comprehensiveness[7] and insisted on including a general **principle of flexibility** that might allow them to placate certain sensitive sectors (particularly agriculture) by putting them on a slower timetable or possibly even exclude them from complete liberalization. This attempt by the Japan-led group to provide flexibility for sensitive sectors had been rebuffed by the other APEC senior officials in both the July and October 1995 meetings. The United States and twelve APEC members viewed the principle of comprehensiveness as vital to achieving the Bogor vision of free trade in APEC. In Osaka, APEC members reached a compromise that allowed the comprehensiveness principle to remain unchanged but added the principle of flexibility.[8] Japan reportedly hops to interpret the flexibility principle to mean that it may postpone liberalizing its rice market until close to the year 2010. By then, many of its elderly rice farmers will have retired.

[7] October 25, 1995, Representatives Doug Bereuter and Howard L. Berman along with 27 other Members of the U.S. House of Representatives sent a letter to Secretary of State Warren Christopher and USTR Mickey Kantor urging the Administration not to weaken its resolve to press for "the promised comprehensive and detailed agenda for implementing the Bogor Declaration."

[8] The flexibility principle reads: Considering the different levels of economic development among the APEC economies and the diverse circumstances in each economy, flexibility will be available in dealing with issues arising from such circumstances in the liberalization and facilitation process.

At Osaka, Malaysia also argued for making all APEC commitments "voluntary" (meaning that the free-trade target dates would not be binding). For the Bogor Declaration, Malaysia had attached its objections to establishing the goal of free trade and investment by the year 2010 or 2020. As a compromise, the word "voluntary" was added. The Osaka Leaders' Declaration stated APEC's resolve to "encourage...the evolving efforts of **voluntary liberalization** in the region," but the Osaka Action Agenda clearly declared under the comprehensiveness principle that "the APEC liberalization and facilitation process will be comprehensive, addressing all impediments to achieving the long-term goal of free and open trade and investment."[9] Japan's trade Minister Ryutaro Hashimoto, who had argued for flexibility, stated clearly in a news conference announcing the declaration that the dates and commitments for free trade stood -- voluntary or not.[10]

APEC members also disagreed over the **non-discrimination principle** or what has been termed "open regionalism." Japan has pressed for the benefits of APEC trade liberalization to be accorded even non-APEC trading partners on a most-favored-nation basis. Japan's Government has stated that it thought APEC should not be a trading bloc that discriminates against outsiders. The problem with such unilateral trade liberalization, however, is that it invites free riders and makes generating public support difficult. The United States favored benefits to be accorded non-APEC countries on a reciprocal basis which has been the basis for other negotiations.[11] The APEC Declaration in Osaka emphasized its "resolute opposition to an inward-looking trading bloc" and committed itself to "firmly maintaining open regional cooperation.: The arguably implies that benefits would be applied non-discriminately among APEC nations, but they would be extended to others only on a reciprocal basis. The Action Agenda stated that "the outcome of trade and investment liberalization...will be the actual reduction of barriers not only among APEC economies but also between APEC economies and non-APEC economies."[12]

China has been insisting that non-discrimination in APEC means that it be ensured **most-favored-nation** (MFN) trading status by the United States. U.S. law, however, requires that China's MFN status be reviewed annually.[13] The compromise wording crafted for the Osaka Action Agenda was that "APEC

[9] APEC Osaka Action Agenda, p. 1.

[10] Tarrant, Bill. APEC Dodges Bullet, Keeps Free Trade Plan Momentum. Reuters Newswire Service, November 17, 1995.

[11] Johnstone, Christopher B. An Awkward Dance: The Osaka Summit, Japanese Leadership and the Future of APEC. *JEI Report*, October 20, 1995. p. 12.

[12] APEC Osaka Action Agenda, p. 1.

[13] U.S. Library of Congress. Congressional Research Service. *Most-Favored-Nation Status of the People's Republic of China*. CRS Issue Brief No. IB92094, December 4, 1995 (updated regularly). Washington, 1995. 9p.

members will apply or endeavor to apply the principle of non-discrimination between and among them in the process of liberalization and facilitation of trade and investment." According to U.S. Trade Representative Mickey Kantor, that bit of semantics was "just perfect" for the United States. China indicated that the wording was too vague to resolve the dispute.[14]

In terms of political feasibility, a key question remains to be answered. Would the public support a free trade area encompassing all major Asian and Pacific economies? In the United States, considering the acrimonious debate over implementing the North American Free Trade Agreement, how would the American people respond to a free-trade area that included China, Japan, and South Korea? Import-sensitive industries, such as textiles and apparel, also would likely oppose free imports from Asia.

APEC now is at a critical juncture. After six years of existence, many in the private sector are waiting for concrete measures that will facilitate trade rather than just having discussions and signing declarations. The Osaka meeting did result in enough clear action that APEC seems to have continued its momentum and maintained its credibility and support from business communities throughout the Pacific rim.

APEC'S EVOLUTION AND ACTIVITIES

APEC began in 1989 as an Australian initiative in response to free-trade areas which had developed in Europe and North America. Originally intended to exclude the United States and Canada, APEC was to provide an institution and forum for consultation and coordination on economic issues of importance to East Asia and Australia/New Zealand. Ultimately, however, membership was expanded to encompass North America.

Membership in APEC initially included twelve countries but has now grown to eighteen. The founding members were the United States, Canada, Japan, South Korea, ASEAN (Brunei, Indonesia, Malaysia, Philippines, Singapore, and Thailand, but not Vietnam), Australia, and New Zealand. In 1991, the People's Republic of China, Taiwan, and Hong Kong joined. In 1993, Mexico and Papua New Guinea were admitted, as was Chile in 1994. Additional membership decisions have been deferred until 1996 when applications from Vietnam, Russia, India, Mongolia, Panama, and other countries may be considered.

APEC symbolized post-Cold War relationships in which trade and investment have become an important pillar in the foundation underlying world peace and security. While trade still may be used as a punitive measure in U.S. foreign

[14]Sieg, Linda. U.S. Trade Envoy Says APEC Has Reached "Good" Deal. Reuters News Service. November 16, 1995.

policy, it also may become a catalyst for change in countries with authoritarian governments or isolated markets. APEC promotes cooperation and trade among the nations of the Pacific Basin, encourages open trading systems rather than trading blocs, keeps the United States engaged in the region, and provides the Asia Pacific with a counterweight to the European Union. In 1993, support by APEC for concluding the Uruguay Round GATT negotiations placed pressure on Europe that hastened the signing of the final agreement.

APEC is a far cry from either the European Union or North American Free Trade Agreement (NAFTA) -- or even AFTA, the ASEAN Free Trade Area. APEC's goal of free trade is to be phased in over the next quarter century. Only the framework now exists to lead APEC members toward that goal. APEC is not a negotiating body nor are its decisions legally binding on its members. APEC
s staff is modest, and its consensus-based decisionmaking is cumbersome. Rather than a trade bloc, it may serve as a building block toward greater trade liberalization and cooperation world wide.

In terms of APEC activities, the annual **Leaders Meeting** is attended by heads of state except for those from Taiwan and Hong Kong (because of China's objections). Although APEC confines its agenda to economic issues, the heads of state at bilateral meetings conducted before and after the "summit" have discussed concerns over international security, human rights, and other issues. The 1996 Leaders Meeting is to be held in The Philippines, the 1997 meeting in Canada, and the 1998 meeting in Malaysia.[15]

The annual **Joint Ministerial Meeting** preceding the Leaders Meeting is attended by foreign, trade, and some commerce ministers from member states. The chair of both the Ministerial and Leaders' Meetings is held by the host country. Management of substance is handled under ministerial direction through Senior Officials Meetings. Specialized APEC ministerial meetings also are held. In 1993, APEC created a secretariat in Singapore with an Executive Director, 40-person staff, and a modest budget ($2.8 million in 1986). In 1995, Japan indicated that it would provide APEC with 10 billion yen (about $100 million) to fund APEC cooperative projects.[16]

Most of the specific tasks facing APEC are being addressed in committees or working groups that deal with economic issues of importance to the region. These include the Committee on Trade and Investment, the Economic Committee, and the following working groups: (1) Trade and Investment Data, (2) Trade Promotion, (3) Industrial Science and Technology, (4) Human Resources Development, (5) Energy Cooperation, (6) Marine Resource Conservation, (7) Tele-

---

[15] In December 1996, the Flag Desecration Constitutional Amendment was held up in the Senate because of a threatened filibuster because the Senate had not acted on the appointments of several ambassadors, including the U.S. Ambassador to APEC.

[16] Japan to Offer 10 Billion Yen for APEC Trade liberalization. Dow Jones Newswire Service, November 14, 1995.

communications, (8) Transportation, (9) Tourism, and (10) Fisheries. The groups develop activities aimed at expanding economic cooperation among members. Each working group has one or more shepherds (members) who take responsibility for coordinating the work of the group.

In 1992, APEC formed the Eminent Persons Group (EPG) and charged it with developing a "vision" for APEC's future. In 1994, the EPG recommended that APEC establish the goal of free trade, and, in 1995, recommended ways to achieve that vision. The EPG completed its task in 1995. In 1994, APEC also formed the Pacific Business Forum to provide a channel for private sector interests to be expressed.[17] For the United States, this would normally require consideration under fast-track authority for approval of trade agreements.

In 1995, U.S. Defense Secretary William Perry started a debate about whether APEC should be expanded to include consideration of regional security issues. Heretofore, all such discussions were confined to bilateral summit meetings surrounding the Leaders Meetings. APEC has carefully kept its distance from security matters for fear that such issues would cause divisions within the group -- particularly between China and other members, such as Taiwan, the United States, and Japan. Such divisions could thwart cooperation in achieving economic goals. The consensus in 1995, seemed to be that regional security issues should be discussed in the ASEAN Regional Forum rather than in APEC.[18] The ASEAN Regional Forum usually meets after the ASEAN Ministerial Conference and, in addition to the seven members of ASEAN, includes the United States, China, Russia, Japan, South Korea, Australia, New Zealand, Canada, and the European Union. It provides the largest pan-Pacific forum for discussing security issues.[19]

THE APEC REGION AND TRADE

The Asia Pacific region contains nearly half the world's population, 60 percent of the world's gross domestic product, and 40 percent of its trade. U.S. trade with APEC nations, even excluding Canada and Mexico, is twice as great as that with the European Union. In the near term, Asian markets (except for Japan's) are expected to grow more rapidly than those in North America or Europe. Since the U.S. market already is relatively open, Americans stand to gain more from the lowering of trade barriers abroad than other countries have in further reductions

---

17 [U.S. Department of State]. *APEC 1995, A Guide for the Perplexed*. Washington, 1995. 18P. See: Eminent Persons Group. *Achieving the APEC Vision, Free and Open trade in the Asia Pacific*. Singapore, APEC Secretariat, 1995. Pacific Business Forum. *The Osaka Action Plan: Roadmap to Realising the APEC Vision*. Asia-Pacific Economic Cooperation, 1995. 57p.

18 Moosa, Eugene. Regional Security Remains a Taboo at APEC. Reuters Newswire Service. November 19, 1995.

19 U.S. Library of Congress. Congressional Research Service. *Regional Security Consultative Organizations in East Asia and Their Implications for the United States*. CRS Report No. 94-79, by Larry Niksch. Washington, 1994. 15p.

in such barriers in the United States. Import duties on automobiles in Southeast Asia, for example, range from 30 to 60 percent compared with 2.5 percent in the United States.

U.S. trade with most of these Asian countries, however, is highly unbalanced. In 1994, of the $151 billion U.S. deficit in merchandise trade with the world, $130 billion of 86 percent was with APEC Asia. In short, in as much as the U.S. trade deficit is a problem, that problem largely centers around the Asian APEC member countries. (See table 1.)

TABLE 1. U.S. Merchandise Trade with APEC Nations/Groups, 1994 ($ million)

Nation/Group	U.S. Exports	U.S. Imports	Balance	Trade Deficit as % of Total US Trade Deficit
Japan	53,481	119,149	-65,668	43.4%
South Korea	18,028	19,658	-1,630	1.1%
China/Hong Kong	20,732	48,479	-27,747	18.3%
Taiwan	17,078	26,711	-9,633	6.4%
Total Chinese	37,810	75,190	-37.380	24.7%
Economic Area	109,319	213,997	-104,678	69.1%
Total NE Asia	376	46	330	-0.2%
Brunei	2,811	6,523	-3,712	2.5%
Indonesia	6,965	13,977	-7,012	4.6%
Malaysia	13,022	15,360	-2,338	1.5%
Singapore	4,861	10,307	-5,446	3.6%
Thailand	3,888	5,720	-1,832	1.2%
Philippines	172	50	122	-0.1%
Vietnam	32,095	51,983	-19,888	13.1%
Total ASEAN	141,414	265,980	-124,566	82.3%
Total NE	9,781	3,200	6,581	-4.3%
Asia/ASEAN	1.508	1,421	87	-0.1%
Australia	2,776	1,822	954	-0.6%
New Zealand	65	108	-43	0.0%
Chile	320,467	450,921	-130,454	86.2%
Papua New Guinea	165,095	178,440	-13,345	8.8%
Total APEC	512,416	663,830	-151,414	100.0%
Total NAFTA				
Total World				

Note: N.A. = not applicable. NAFTA includes the United States, Canada, and Mexico
Source: Data are from U.S. Department of Commerce

Despite the great amount of trade and economic growth in the Asia Pacific region, only four trading arrangements currently exist among APEC countries. The North American Free Trade Agreement, the agreement for Closer Economic Relations between Australian and New Zealand, the ASEAN Free Trade Area (that reduces but does not eliminate trade barriers within ASEAN by the year

2003), and the Chile-Mexican Free Trade Agreement. The United States, however, has agreed to complete negotiations to create a Free Trade Area of the Americas by the year 2005. Negotiations for Chile to join NAFTA also began in 1995.[20] In response to APEC, the European Union has floated the idea of a trans-Atlantic free-trade agreement. In 1995, this was considered but dropped. On December 3, 1995, however, the United States and the European Union announced a New Transatlantic Agenda which includes a goal of creating a New Transatlantic Marketplace aimed at reducing barriers to trade.[21]

Japan and its neighboring Asian economies, however, are building trade and investment networks that could develop into a powerful trading bloc, if organized. Japanese and Chinese production networks have been proliferating in East and Southeast Asia. Japan also has been increasing the percentage of its trade that is conducted in yen, although a yen block steel seems quite distant. Trade friction, moreover, has induced many of the Asian nations to diversity their exports away from the U.S. market and toward each other.

A key difference between APEC and the European Union of NAFTA is the degree of diversity among member states. APEC members range from locations encompassing the Gobi Desert in the north to Cape Horn in the south with populations ranging from the 1.2 billion people in China to the 268,000 in Brunei, and spanning the economic development spectrum from the industrial giants of the United States and Japan to the newly industrialized economies such as South Korea and Singapore on to poor nations such as Papua New Guinea. Cultures range from European to Asian and to Latin American. Religions, types of governments, economic systems, and average educational levels, likewise, differ greatly.

EAST ASIAN ECONOMIC CAUCUS

The momentum in APEC along with Japan's reluctance to risk offending the United States has sidelined a proposal by Malaysian Prime Minister Mahathir to form an East Asian Economic Caucus, a consultative caucus within APEC. Membership would include only Asia members of APEC and would provide a forum for Asian nations to coordinate policies and provide Japan with Asian points of view before multilateral meetings, such as the G-7. The Bush Administration opposed the creation of the EAEC directly, while the Clinton Administration has been highly skeptical of it. Without Japan's participation, the EAEC is not likely to be organized.

---

[20] U.S. Library of Congress. Congressional Research Service. *Trade and the Americas*. CRS Issue Brief No. IB95017, November 29, 1995 (updated regularly). Washington, 1995. 16p.

[21] U.S. Department of State. The New Transatlantic Agenda. Fact Sheet. November 30, 1995.

In order to circumvent U.S. objections, in December 1996, ASEAN plans an informal summit with itself and the countries invited to join the EAEC. The idea is for ASEAN leaders to meet with other East Asian heads of state to discuss issues. ASEAN claims such a caucus would be no different from other caucuses which exist elsewhere in the world.[22] Whether or not other East Asian leaders will attend and whether this will be viewed as the launch of an EAEC-type of organization is yet to be seen.

APPENDIX A: SUMMARY OF OSAKA INITIAL ACTIONS

The following is a summary of initial actions announced by APEC members in Osaka on November 19, 1995, for liberalization and facilitation of trade and investment. These actions represent the first wide-ranging initiatives by APEC members to use the organization to accelerate the implementation of their Uruguay Round commitments, to deepen and broaden the outcomes of the Uruguay Round, and to launch deregulation measures.

AUSTRALIA: To open its telecommunications sector to competition from July 1, 1997. Advancing tariff cuts offered in Uruguay Round of global trade talks so that final bound rates for industrial products will be achieved in 1998 and on agricultural products in 1999.

BRUNEI: Submitted previously announced proposals to reduce tariffs on 688 items. To amend trademarks and copyright laws.

CANADA: Submitted previously announced measures to reduce 1,500 tariff lines and extended NAFTA preferential investment provisions to all investors.

CHILE: Bringing forward implementation of tariff commitments across the board and eliminating trade distortive agricultural support measures.

CHINA: From 1996, to slash overall tariffs by an average of 30 percent on more than 4,000 tariff lines. Pledged to eliminate quota, licensing and other import control measures on about 170 tariff lines accounting for more than 30 percent of the commodities now subject to such quotas and licensing requirements. Designated Shanghai and other cities as pilot bases for Sino-foreign joint ventures.

HONG KONG: To place an additional five percent of its imports in the duty-free category, to decontrol telecom and financial sectors.

INDONESIA: Submitted previously announced reductions on 96 percent of all tariffs exceeding 5 percent and is accelerating the elimination of non-tariff barriers faster than required under the Uruguay Round accord.

JAPAN: Bringing forward tariff cuts on 697 industrial and mining products. Announced 50 deregulatory measures, including easing visa restrictions for business executives,

---

[22] ASEAN Plans 'Virtual' EAEC Meeting At 'Informal' Summit Next Year. *The Daily Japan Digest*, December 14, 1996. p. 1-2.

SOUTH KOREA: After liberalizing 53 additional businesses for foreign investments in 1995, is liberalizing 89 more in 1996, 38 more in 1997, and 21 more by 2000. As announced previously, will lower tariffs on automobiles and other items while deregulating railways, food inspections, and customs procedures.

MALAYSIA: As previously announced, accelerated cuts in tariffs on 2,317 items in 1995 and 1,047 items in 1996, liberalizing financial services, capital markets, telecommunications, electricity and shipping.

MEXICO: Submitted previously announced proposals liberalizing foreign investment in railroads, satellite communications, natural gas distribution, transportation and financial services.

NEW ZEALAND: Unilaterally reducing tariffs so about half will be zero with the rest no higher than 15 percent by 2000. To implement agreement in intellectual property rights ahead of schedule.

PAPUA NEW GUINEA: Negotiating to join the World Trade Organisation. Will cut tariffs and dismantle non-tariff barriers.

PHILIPPINES: Will lower all tariffs to 5 percent by 2004 and ease regulations on foreign investment under previously announced measures.

SINGAPORE: Will accelerate Uruguay Round tariff reductions. Will implement agreements on intellectual property and investment measures ahead of schedule; to deregulate state-run employee pension fund, telecommunications, and electricity sectors.

TAIWAN: Cutting tariffs on 758 items, relaxing bans and quotas on some imported goods and opening more sectors to foreign investment.

THAILAND: Accelerated cuts on 25 percent of the tariff items in its Uruguay Round commitments. Opening up its financial services sector and setting up an intellectual property and trade court.

UNITED STATES: Relaxing customs procedures and export controls and streamlining government procurement practices under previously announced measures.

Australia, New Zealand, and the Pacific Islands

Robert G. Sutter

Summary

U.S. interests and policy concerns in the vast region known as Oceania have changed in recent years. U.S. concern to secure naval and other access to and through the region grew in the 1980s as a result of New Zealand's anti-nuclear policies and concurrent Soviet efforts to expand its influence and probe for Western vulnerabilities. In the post-Cold War environment, security issues may no longer take precedence over a range of other policy problems for U.S. leaders.

Security concerns focus on maintaining a close U.S.-Australian alliance in a post Cold War environment; possible improvements in U.S.-New Zealand relations; issues stemming from U.S. refusal to sign the South Pacific Nuclear Free Zone Treaty and from France's nuclear weapons testing program in French Polynesia; and signs of political instability among some of the small Pacific Island States.

Economic issues relate to discord in U.S. relations with Australia over competing agricultural and other trade practices; a 10-year U.S. Pacific Island tuna fishing agreement; and very limited U.S. development assistance efforts at a time of poor economic prospects for island states.

Political issues include determining the scope and level of U.S. Government attention to the region and U.S. policy on sensitive self-determination and political autonomy questions, especially for New Caledonia and Papua New Guinea.

Environmental problems relate to France's nuclear testing program, U.S. plans to destroy chemical weapons in the Pacific, and U.S. efforts to work with the countries of Oceania in dealing with such problems as driftnet fishing and potential global warning.

Through its oversight, funding, and advisory powers, Congress continues to play an important role in determining U.S. policy in the region. Some in Congress have urged the United States to be more active in significant issues related to Oceania. Some want the Administration to go further in meeting regional concerns and improving relations with regional actors. But others warn of substantial negative consequences for U.S. policy if American leaders focus on regional concerns to the detriment of other U.S. interests.

In recent years, the combination of U.S. preoccupation with domestic and other foreign policy issues and restricted Government spending has prompted scaled-down American Government efforts in Oceania.

U.S. Interests in Oceania

U.S. interests and policy concerns in this vast region have changed in recent years. After World War II, the United States for several decades followed a passive policy, relying partly on Western colonial powers, Australia, and New Zealand to maintain the largely unchallenged U.S. interest in unimpeded military access to the region. Developments in Oceania were seen to be generally favorable to American interests. For the most part, democratically elected governments controlled the region, encouraged free market economic development, and were friendly toward the United States. These governments served U.S. interests by allowing U.S. warships and aircraft to be based in, stop at, and pass through their territory, and by rebuffing repeated Soviet efforts to gain influence in the region. As a result, the United States enjoyed secure lines of communication through Oceania to Asia, the Indian Ocean, and the Persian Gulf. (For background and more detail on issues treated here, see **FOR ADDITIONAL READING.**)

In the mid-1980s, New Zealand's new anti-nuclear policies had a serious impact on military and security cooperation under the U.S.-Australian-New Zealand (ANZUS) alliance --- the linchpin of the U.S.-backed collective security in the region. The U.S.-New Zealand leg of the alliance became moribund. The Soviet Union also played a more active diplomatic and commercial role with the sometimes unstable, recently independent Pacific Island countries. U.S. policy became more active in considering ways to secure military access and other interests.

The demise of the Cold War and other recent developments have given U.S. policy a decidedly less military cast. Today, American interests and policy concerns remain active but are dispersed over a range of security, economic, political, and environmental concerns. Many of the issues relate to only one or a few of the over 20 states, territories, or other political entities that are included in Oceania. These countries range in size from the continent of Australia, having a population of 18 million, to the many Pacific Island states with relatively small populations that are often crowded into limited land areas. Despite these differences, the countries often work together through regional groups, notably the 16-member South Pacific Forum (see **Table 1**), in putting forth a collective view on issues to outside powers, including the United States.

At present, the United States maintains military based in the U.S. territory of Guam. There used to be three major so-called "joint facilities" used by the

United States in Australia (one of the three -- Northwest Cape -- was transferred to Australian command on Oct. 1, 1992). The United States also leases an important missile test site at Kwajalein, in the Marshall Islands, and leases territory for possible future military use in the Northern Mariana Islands.

The United States continues extensive government programs in the U.S. insular areas of Guam, the Northern Mariana Islands, Federated States of Micronesia, and Palau. (See CRS Report 92-477 GOV, *Political Development of U.S. Insular Areas*.) Elsewhere in the Pacific, the United States had relied mainly on the diplomatic and aid efforts of Australia, New Zealand, Japan, and Great Britain to support mutually pursued interests, help the resource-poor island countries maintain basic government services, and promote economic development.

TABLE 1. Members of the South Pacific Forum

Country	Size[a]	Population	Economy per capita[b]
Australia	7,600,000	18,077,419	$19,100
Cook Islands	240	19,124	3,000
F.S. of Micronesia	720	120,347	1,500
Fiji	18,270	764,382	4,000
Kiribati	717	77,853	525
Marshall Islands	181	54,031	1,500
Nauru	21	10,019	10,000
New Zealand	268,680	3,388,737	15,700
Niue	260	1,906	1,000
Papua New Guinea	461,690	4,196,806	2,000
Solomon Islands	28,450	385,811	2,500
Tonga	748	104,778	2,000
Tuvalu	26	9,831	700
Vanuatu	14,760	169,776	1,050
Western Samoa	2,860	204,447	2,000

Source: CIA, The World Factbook, 1994.
a. Size expressed in square and kilometers.
b. Economic figures represent dollars per capita gross domestic product.

According to the U.S. AID, in FY1994, the allocation of U.S. aid to countries in the region (including the multi-million dollar U.S. fisheries accords: (see below) amounted to about $21 million. For FY1995, it was about $14 million. The administration's request for FY1996 was about $14 million.

U.S. trade with Oceania is only a small fraction of overall U.S. foreign trade. American tuna fishing fleets use regional fishing grounds, including those areas claimed as exclusive economic zones (EEZs) by some island states. American trade negotiators work closely with Australia and New Zealand in promoting a reduction of government subsidies and other impediments to free trade in agricultural commodities. U.S. agricultural subsidies promoting the sale of U.S. grain and daily products abroad are an important bone of contention with Australian farmers and their government representatives. The U.S. Government finds strong support from South Pacific countries whenever it comes out in opposition to driftnet fishing, encouraging international efforts to study and take measures to deal with potential global warming, and restricting acts that would endanger the environment through testing nuclear weapons, destroying chemical weapons, or depositing toxic or other waste in the ocean.

After briefly reviewing U.S. interests in Oceania, this report assesses issues in U.S. relations with Australia, a key U.S. ally and by far the most important country in the region. It then reviews in a thematic way (e.g., political, security, economic, etc.) issues in U.S. relations throughout the region. The narrative concludes with a review of Congress' role and options.

AUSTRALIA-U.S. RELATIONS -- PROBLEMS AND PROSPECTS[1]

Tied together by common political values, close economic relations, and overlapping security interests in Asian-Pacific and world affairs, the United States and Australia maintain a very close alliance relationship. Nevertheless, the post Cold War security environment has reduced the strategic imperative behind the relationship, allowed long-standing trade and other disputes to become more prominent, and raised questions about the degree of commonality in the two countries' approaches to regional and world affairs.

Trade issues have become the most common source of friction in a very close and active bilateral economic relationship. The United States is Australia's second largest trading partner (after Japan) and it runs an almost three to one favorable balance in bilateral trade with Australia. The United States is also the largest source of foreign investment in Australia, and U.S. companies have shown interest in Australia as a site for corporate headquarters dealing with the dynamic economies throughout the Pacific rim.

Australian officials complain about their trade deficit with the United States when it results from what are seen as unfair U.S. trading practices including U.S. nontariff barriers affecting Australian exports of beef, dairy products, steel and sugar. Even more important are disputes over U.S. use of agricultural export subsidies for grain and dairy products. Australians see these actions driving down world prices, including the prices received by Australian exporters, and as taking away markets traditionally services by Australian exporters.

Security ties remain sound. The two countries have a long history of defense cooperation. Their armed forces have served together in both World Wars, Ko-

---

[1]This section is based heavily on the findings from a ten-day study mission to Australia in May-June 1995 that involved close consultations and meetings with over 100 Australian commentators, officials, academics and other opinion leaders.

rea, Vietnam, the Gulf War, and most recently in Somalia. The Joint Defense Facilities are important for mutual security and international arms control efforts. Australia relies heavily on the intelligence it receives as a result of U.S.-Australian intelligence sharing arrangements under the alliance relationship. Australia provides support for U.S. deployments in the Asia-Pacific and Indian Ocean regions through access to ports and airfields, and to maintenance and other support facilities. Australian and U.S. forces exercise and train together on a regular basis. The United States is an important source of high-technology defense equipment for Australia, contributing to Australia's self-reliant defense policy.

The Australian Government's recent emphasis on a "self reliant" defense policy has let it to place less emphasis, at least rhetorically, on the security alliance with the United States. The government's strong efforts in recent years on reorienting the focus of Australia's policy from interests in Europe and North America to those in East and South Asia has also been accompanied by some reduction in attention to the U.S. connection. Reportedly there is some debate among Australian officials as to how much salience to give to the U.S. alliance, although even strong advocates of Australia's recent emphasis on relations with Japan and others in Asia argue that the alliance with the United States is an indispensable ingredient in a successful Australian international posture.

Regional, International issues have seen close Australian-U.S. cooperation, but also some signs of divergence. The Asia-Pacific region accounts for about 70 percent of all Australian trade and approximately 40 percent of all global trade of the United States. Reflecting these vital economic interests, Australia and the United States have played leading roles in the formulation and development of the Asia-Pacific Economic Cooperation (APEC) process. The APEC process is designed to build trust, reduce economic and other barriers, and promote closer cooperation among the Pacific Rim states. Australia and the United States also have worked closely with the Association of Southeast Asian Nations (ASEAN) Regional Forum (ARF) -- a nascent security forum for the Asia-Pacific region.

The Australian Government in recent years has developed a comprehensive policy emphasizing improving relations with the dynamic East Asian economies. It has endeavored to carefully balance Australian concerns over the human rights, disruptive trade practices, assertive military behavior, and other potentially troublesome actions by some Asian countries into a relatively coherent policy approach, with the overall objective of increasing Australia's engagement with the region. In contrast, Australian commentators, academics, and even some officials (usually privately) claim at times to see the United States moving in a different direction. They judge that U.S. officials are less committed than Australians to engagement with Asia, more prone to be distracted by domestic political or other concerns or foreign policy priorities elsewhere, and more likely to allow U.S. concerns with particular issues such as human rights, trade disputes or others to dominate and overcome the broad American interest in closer constructive interaction with the Asian economies.

In mid 1995, for example, Australian commentators were sharply critical of the U.S. efforts to threaten sanctions in order to open the Japanese market to U.S. autos and auto parts. While acknowledging that Japan's market is more closed than others, the Australian commentators highlighted the "selfishness" of the U.S.-proposed solution, noting that if Japan agreed to the American demands it would likely damage auto and auto part suppliers from other countries, including Australia.

The Australian commentators and other observers went further to criticize the U.S. actions because of how it endangered, in their view, the recent international agreements establishing the World Trade Organization. In general, Australian observers averred, the United States places less emphasis and importance on such international organizations than does Australia. They added that the recent sharp decline in U.S. support for UN peacekeeping efforts is greeted with concern in Australia where opinion tends to be supportive of such international ventures.

Political Relations

Leaders of Oceania for many years often saw the United States following a policy of benign neglect toward the region. In the 1980s, with New Zealand's new anti-nuclear policies and more active Soviet diplomatic and commercial initiatives in the area. U.S. policy became more attentive against possible threats to U.S. naval power in the western Pacific and military access to Oceania. Critics in the region held that this did little to address Oceania's economic, development, and environmental concerns. Advocates for a more "effective" U.S. policy argues for an increased U.S. involvement at various levels -- a presence that would allow the United States Government to hear better regional view and adjust U.S. policy where appropriate.

With the support and encouragement of a bipartisan group in Congress concerned with Pacific Island and Oceanian affairs, the Bush Administration took important measures to address these problems. In general, the Administration worked to use diplomacy and greater interchange over security, economic, environmental, and other issues to promote U.S. relations, without requiring a substantial increase in U.S. Government expenditures devoted to the region.[2] The Clinton Administration has shown interest in some of these efforts but, on the whole, U.S. attention to the South Pacific has declined in recent years.

- President Bush became the first U.S. President to visit Australia since the 1960's in December 1991 - January 1992.

[2]See among others, Dorrance, John, *The United States and the Pacific Islands*, Praeger, Westport, CT, 1992, 192 p.

- In October 1990, President Bush became the first U.S. President to hold a summit meeting with 11 Pacific Island leaders.
- A senior U.S. delegation headed by the Assistant Secretary of State for East Asian and Pacific Affairs participated actively in the August 1991 South Pacific Forum's Post-Forum Dialogue and in the Forum Dialogue in August 1993. In July 1991, the United States paid 20 percent of its arrearage to the South Pacific Commission, a regional organization that advises and assists in advancing economic, medical, and social development in Oceania.
- The U.S. diplomatic presence in the Pacific Islands doubled for a time to include six embassies covering Papua New Guinea, Fiji, Federated States of Micronesia, Marshall Islands, Solomon Islands, and Western Samoa. (Funding shortages in 1993 saw proposals to close some of these posts. The post in the Solomon Islands closed in September 1993.)
- Bush Administration initiatives with the Pacific Islands included four new Agency for International Development projects (discussed below) and efforts to use the U.S. Information Agency's international visitor and other programs to send Pacific Island sub-cabinet and cabinet level officials to the United states. On January 12, 1993, the United States and officials from 13 Pacific Island countries signed a memorandum of understanding establishing the U.S.-Pacific Island Nations Joint Commercial Commission. The commission held its first formal session in Washington in October 1993.

On the whole, countries in Oceania welcomes U.S. policy attention and have encourages more.

FRENCH OVERSEAS TERRITORIES[3]

In the past, south pacific forum countries have looked to the United States to support them in their opposition to French administration of the mineral-rich French Overseas Territory of New Caledonia. In August 1986, Forum members urged the United Nations General Assembly to reinscribe the French possession in its list of Non-Self-Governing Territories. France lobbied against this move and attempted to enlist the support of the United States. In general, U.S. policy strove to avoid taking sides in the disputes.

Internal tensions in New Caledonia made it difficult for the United States to maintain its neutral stance. A sometimes violent split developed in the territory between proponents of continued French rule and those favoring full independence. The split tended to follow ethnic lines, with native Melanesians favoring independence and settlers from France favoring continued French rule. The de-

[3]For background information, see among others, Christopher, Luella S., *Pacific Island Nations: Overview of Trends and Problems in the South and West Pacific*, CRS Report 90-396 F, Washington, July 29, 1990, 30 p.

mands of the native Melanesians, led by the Kanak Socialist National Liberation Front, were supported by Melanesian states and Australia and New Zealand. The demands of the Kanak Front met a firm response from the French administration of conservative then-Prime Minister Jacques Chirac. After French elections in May 1988, the new French government seemed more accommodating. A compromise was reached in August 1988 and approved by French voters on November 6, 1988. It called for a referendum on a new federal system in 1988 and one on possible self-determination for the territory 10 years later. The compromise helped to improve French relations with South pacific Forum countries and reduced the policy dilemma for the United States. Nevertheless, regional concerns over French territories arose anew in the 1990s as a result of a movement in French Polynesia calling for greater local autonomy and self-determination.

PALAU

This 200-island area was one of our parts of a strategic U.N. trust territory administered by the United States. The others were the Northern Mariana Islands, the Federated States of Micronesia (FSM), and the Marshall Islands. Agreements with three of the four governments were negotiated in the 1970s and 1980s. Micronesia and the Marshall Islands became sovereign states in free association with the United States through a compact. The Northern Mariana Islands became a commonwealth in union with and under the sovereignty of the United States through a covenant. Arrangements with the Marshall Islands and the Federated States of Micronesia have been approved by Congress and the United Nations and are being implemented by the United States.

The terms of the compact with Palau allow U.S. nuclear-capable warships to transit Palau and allow the use of military facilities for 50 years. The compact failed to be approved in seven referenda although it was supported in each by a majority of Palau voters. Palau's constitution, however, required that the compact be approved by a 75-percent majority because the agreement would grant the United States nuclear rights that would conflict with current provisions of Palau's constitution. In a November 1992 vote, Palau voters approved a constitutional amendment to reduce from a 75-percent majority to a simple majority the vote margin needed to amend anti-nuclear provisions of the constitution. A November 9, 1993, referendum on the compact passed by a 68- to 32-percent margin. On October 1, 1994, Palau ended its status as a trust territory and became an independent, sovereign state. The United States, Japan, and Australia were among the first to recognize the new government.[4]

---

[4]For background, see among others, Luella Christopher, *Pacific Island Nations and the United States: Developing a Closer Dialogue*, CRS Report 90-541 F, Washington, October 23, 1990, 35 p; and Robert Sutter and Matthew Sakrekoff, *Palau: Briefing Paper*. CRS Report 95-40 S, Washington, December 23, 1994, 2p.

PAPUA NEW GUINEA

Separatist conflicts from time to time threaten the unity of some newly independent Pacific Island states. A bitter and often violent separatist conflict involving people on the island of Bougainville in Papua New Guinea (PNG) has gone on for several years. On September 4, 1994, the government and rebel representatives signed a peace accord to be monitored by peacekeepers from South Pacific Forum (SPF) countries. By October 1994, the accord broke down and the SPF peacekeepers withdrew from Bougainville. The United States has not been pressed to play an active role in the conflict, which has involved PNG, its former administrator and largest aid giver, Australia, the Solomon Islands (a neighbor of Bougainville often critical of PNG and Australia over this issue), and other Pacific Forum countries.

SECURITY POLICY

Specific issues for U.S. security policy have focused on nuclear issues. New Zealand's anti-nuclear policies led to the suspension by the United States of military and security cooperation with New Zealand under ANZUS. A broadly popular move in the region would create a South Pacific nuclear free zone and halt French nuclear weapons testing in French Polynesia. Also, regional instability might be exploited by outside powers adverse to U.S. interests.

Taking a stand strongly opposed to U.S. and other states' nuclear weapons in Oceania, a Labor Party government took power in New Zealand in 1984 and eventually, in 1987, pushed through legislation banning nuclear weapons and nuclear-powered warships from New Zealand. In response, the U.S. suspended military alliance relations and reduced other government contacts to a low level. President Bush began in 1990 and 1991 to resume a few high-level contacts. The President's decision in late 1991 to remove nuclear weapons from U.S. ships except ballistic missile submarines may have helped to east U.S.-New Zealand differences. New Zealand is willing to welcome U.S. warships that are not nuclear powered and do not carry nuclear weapons, but over 40-percent of U.S. naval combatant ships are nuclear powered. On December 17, 1992, a New Zealand government-commissioned report found that nuclear-powered ships pose no threat and should be allowed to visit the country. The Clinton Administration in February 1994 resumed high-level contacts with New Zealand, but security and intelligence ties remain on hold.[5]

A treaty declaring the South pacific to be a nuclear free zone was signed by South Pacific Forum members in 1985. The treaty has three protocols which the Forum has asked the United States and other nuclear powers to sign. The Soviet Union and China signed the protocols of the treaty in late 1986 and early 1987, respectively. the Reagan Administration announced in February 1987 that the

[5] See among others, *The Washington Times*, February 25, 1994, p. 16.

United States would not sign the protocols. Great Britain also announced that it would not sign the protocols. The Clinton Administration is in the process of reviewing the U.S. position on the treaty and its protocols.

The treaty reserves for each South Pacific country the right to decide whether to limit naval and air access to its territory, but it poses several potential problems for the United States. In particular, it precludes the stationing or permanent emplacement of nuclear weapons in Australia, New Zealand, and the Pacific island states south of the equator. (U.S. officials strongly emphasize that the United States has no interest in such nuclear capability.) Signing the protocols could prompt other countries to demand U.S. endorsement of nuclear free zones in some other, more sensitive regions of the world (e.g., Europe, Northeast Asia, the Middle East).

By signing the protocols, the United States could be seen as supporting the text of the treaty, which contains strong criticism of French nuclear testing in French Polynesia. France announced, in April 1991, a conditional moratorium on nuclear testing; President Clinton, on July 3, 1993, announced a conditional moratorium on U.S. tests and, on March 16, 1994, notified Congress that he would extend the moratorium for another year. China continued to conduct nuclear tests, but other nuclear powers tuck to their moratoriums until after passage of the renewal of the international treaty on nuclear nonproliferation in 1995. In June 1995, the newly installed French President Chirac decided that France would resume nuclear testing in French Polynesia. The South Pacific Forum countries were joined by the United States in criticizing the move.

U.S. policy in the past worried about Soviet and, to a lesser degree, Libyan efforts to exploit political or military instability among some governments in the Pacific Islands. The diminution of Cold War and other outside threats has reduced U.S. strategic concerns, although the United States continues to work through military, diplomatic, and foreign assistance channels to ease conflicts and promote stability. Regional concerns include Fiji's slow efforts to restore parliamentary democracy after military coups in the 1980s and the political struggles for greater autonomy, separatism, or independence seen in Bougainville, New Caledonia, French Polynesia, and elsewhere.

With civil action projects, disaster relief, joint exercises, training and exchange programs, the U.S. military -- mainly the United States Navy -- has built contacts with many Pacific Island states. The U.S. had status of forces -- agreements with several Pacific Island States (e.g., FSM, Marshall Islands, PNG, Western Samoa, and Solomon Islands). The United States gives small amounts of U.S. military training (IMET) to PNG, Solomon Islands, Tonga, Vanuatu, and Western Samoa.[6]

[6]For background, see CRS Issue Brief 92044, *Australia, new Zealand and the Pacific Islands*, archived, October 27, 1994.

ECONOMIC ISSUES

The issues for U.S. policy focus on U.S.-Australian discord over agricultural trade and practices, bilateral aviation disputes, the U.S.-Pacific Island fishing agreement, and U.S. economic policy initiatives and United States assistance to Pacific Island states. A clear distinction exists between U.S. economic issues with Australia and, to a lesser degree, New Zealand, which center on trade disputes involving developed countries, and U.S. economic concerns with the smaller, less developed Pacific Island countries, which focus on U.S. assistance to development and U.S. use of local resources, especially tuna fish.

The U.S. Government Export Enhancement Program (EEP) is designed to promote U.S. agricultural sales abroad. Australian farmers and their representatives say that those sales come at the expense of Australian sales in world markets and that the subsidies have an overall effect of lowering prices for agricultural commodities. The United States has argued that such efforts were needed to counter the heavily subsidized agricultural trade by members of the European Community (EC) and to encourage the EC to reach compromises on agricultural trade at the Uruguay Round negotiations of the GATT, which were favored by both the United States and Australia.

Many of the small Pacific Island states depend heavily on income derived from fishing, claiming rights to the fishing resources in large maritime economic zones -- known as Exclusive Economy Zones (EEZs) -- around their territory. Most countries recognize such zones, which are covered by the Law of the Sea convention. In the past, the United Sates took the position that the zones, extending 200 miles from the island states' land area, did not apply to tuna, a highly migratory fish species. As a result, American tuna fishing fleets were perceived as repeatedly violating the claimed rights of several Pacific Island governments, and some governments seized and fined U.S. tuna boats. (This position was reversed with enactment of P.L. 101-627, wherein the U.S. extended jurisdiction over highly migratory species.)

The U.S. Government attempted to ease the problem by negotiating a regional fisheries agreement. The accord, in the form of a treaty, was signed on April 2, 1987. Under its terms, the United States agreed to a $12-million annual financial package, made up of $2 million from the U.S. tuna fishing industry ($1.75 million in license fees for 35 boats in the first year, plus $.25 million in technical assistance) and $10 million in U.S. aid. A U.S. Government assistance package was divided between $9 million in aid grants and $1 million to project assistance. The Senate ratified the treaty on November 6, 1987. The treaty went into effect on June 15, 1988. The Administration and Congress followed through with the $10 million in annual aid required under the treaty.

President Bush announced in October 1990 that the United States would seek to negotiate to extend the treaty; these negotiations were completed in May 1992. The accord was to be approved by the countries concerned, including the

United States, but it was said not to require Senate ratification. It involves a 10-year extension of the previous 5-year agreement, including annual payments of $14 million and $4 million by the U.S. Government and U.S. fishing industry, respectively. The U.S. Administration allocated $14 million for this purpose in the FY1993 aid budget and the same amount for later years.

On development questions, the Bush Administration focused on initiatives announced at the October 1990 Honolulu summit. These included the foundation of a Joint commercial Commission (JCC) between the United States and independent Pacific Island nations (a memorandum of understanding on the JCC was signed by the United States and 13 Pacific Island nations on January 12, 1993, and meetings of the JCC were held in October 1993); a more active role for the Overseas Private Investment Corporation and the U.S. Export-Import Bank; and U.S. AID efforts to promote commercial agriculture, marine resources development, health assistance, and other benefits. U.S. development aid programs ended in the mid-1990s. Over 400 US. Peace Corps volunteers continued to serve in 12 Pacific Island states in the 1990s.[7]

Despite these efforts and the larger aid efforts of Australia, New Zealand, Japan, and others, there remained little optimism in the mid-1990s regarding the economic development of most Pacific Island states. In the main, the countries were too small and isolated from international communications; had poor resources; ineffective, bloated, and/or corrupt governments; and numerous social-environmental problems including overpopulation of available land, rural-urban migration, social dislocation, and substance abuse.[8]

ENVIRONMENTAL ISSUES[9]

Many in Oceania strongly oppose French nuclear weapons testing in French Polynesia on environmental grounds, and are concerned by U.S. refusal to oppose its ally's practice. Ongoing U.S. destruction of chemical weapons at Johnston Island in the Pacific also prompt regional concern. Regional commentators welcome U.S. support for world efforts to curb driftnet fishing, and also support a stronger international effort favored by the Clinton Administration to deal with potential global warming.

Australia, New Zealand, and the other members of the South Pacific Forum repeatedly condemned French nuclear weapons testing; they urged the United States to sign the protocols for the Forum-endorsed treaty creating a South Pacific Nuclear Free Zone and to take other steps that condemn the French testing. Many in the region claim that the French tests, conducted underground in a

---

[7] Reviewed in John Dorrance's, *The United States and the Pacific Islands, op cit.*, Praeger, Westport, CT, 1992, 192 p.

[8] See, among others, speeches by Australia's Pacific Islands minister of October 27, 1994 and June 15, 1994 (available from Australian Embassy, Washington, D.C.).

[9] See, among others, Dorrance, John, *op. cit.*, and Davis, Zachary, *The South Pacific Nuclear Free Zone Treaty*, CRS Report 93-610 ENR, Washington, June 25, 1993, 6 p.

Polynesian atoll, are environmentally unsafe, despite repeated French surveys claiming no danger.

Many Pacific Islanders criticized the U.S. plan in 1990 to destroy on-site chemical weapons stored on the U.S. territory, Johnston Island -- located several hundred miles southwest of Hawaii -- as well as chemical weapons being shipped to the island from West Germany for that purpose. U.S. officials have repeatedly attempted to reassure their regional counterparts that the chemical weapons destruction program is environmentally safe. On August 10, 1992, a South Pacific Forum scientific mission said the Johnston Island chemical disposal system was safe. The *National Journal* reported, on September 12, 1992, that disposal of the stockpile may take many years longer than anticipated.

The United States took several major steps to show its shared concern with countries of Oceania about driftnet fishing. On November 14, 1990, the U.S. signed the Wellington Convention for Prohibition of Fishing with Long Driftnets in the South Pacific and on February 25, 1991, it signed Protocol I of the convention. The U.S. ratified the South Pacific Regional Environmental Program convention in May 1991. The United States also strongly supported a U.N. resolution, adopted December 20, 1991, unconditionally banning high-seas driftnetting world-wide after December 31, 1992. On October 4, 1992, Congress passed legislation (H.R. 2152, P.L. 102-582) that put into legislative language provision for U.S. unilateral enforcement supporting he U.N. ban on driftnet fishing.

The Clinton Administration has moved to adjust U.S. environmental policy in ways supported by Pacific Island states. Most notable was President Clinton's July 3, 1993, announcement that he had extended the existing U.S. moratorium on underground nuclear tests. The move was seen likely to add to pressures against France resuming nuclear testing in the South Pacific, and to reduce past U.S. opposition to signing the South Pacific Nuclear Free Zone Treaty protocols; both developments would be welcomed by governments in the region. Meanwhile, on July 29, 1994, the Clinton Administration came out against a controversial plan supported by the Marshall Islands' government but opposed by many others in the region to establish a repository in the Marshall Islands for hi-level nuclear waste and spent fuel.

CONGRESS: ROLE AND OPTIONS

Using its oversight, funding, advisory, and other prerogatives, Congress plays an important role in determining U.S. policy towards the region. In recent years, a small bipartisan group of Members has been encouraging the Administration's more active diplomatic, economic, and other interchanges and has urged congress to provide support through modest increases in representational spending and foreign assistance. Seven members of the House Foreign Affairs Committee showed personal interest in regional issues in an unusual meeting with South Pacific diplomats in Washington on October 19, 1993. Some in Congress urge the

United States to go further in meeting regional concerns. Thus, for example, resolutions calling on the United States to sign the protocols on the South Pacific Nuclear Free Zone treaty passed the House in the 100th and 101st Congresses. A resolution on this topic, H. Con. Res. 111, was introduced in the 103rd Congress on June 11, 1993. It was approved by the House Asian-Pacific Subcommittee on November 16, 1993. Various Members have urged greater U.S. flexibility in political contacts with New Zealand, more attention to regional concerns over U.S. chemical weapons destruction, and greater U.S. leadership on the issue of possible global warming.

Reflecting these kinds of concerns, the House Foreign Affairs Committee report of June 11, 1993, on the International Relations Act of 1993 (H. Rept. 103-126) called for several U.S. steps involving the region, including the following:

- Restoring over $1 million in U.S. development assistance to the region that had been cut in the past 2 years;
- Signing protocols on the south Pacific Nuclear Free Zone Treaty (a resolution, H.Con. Res. 111 (Faleomavaega), was introduced on this subject on June 10);
- Strengthening the U.S. Joint Commercial Commission (JCC) with Pacific Island states;
- Reviewing U.S. restrictions on contacts with New Zealand;
- Reviewing the U.S. decision to close diplomatic posts in the Solomon Islands and Palau; and
- Establishing within USIA active south Pacific exchange programs.

On November 16, 1993, the House Asian-Pacific Subcommittee approved H. Con. Res. 180 calling for more active U.S. Government involvement with South Pacific issues. It passed the House on February 22, 1994. On April 30, 1994, President Clinton signed H.R. 2333 (P.L. 103-236), which has a provision calling for enhanced U.S.-South Pacific Exchange Programs. On May 18, 1994, the House Foreign Affairs Committee reported H. Con. Res. 111, urging U.S. support for the South Pacific Nuclear Free Zone Treaty.

The 104th Congress has seen far less attention to South Pacific issues. Exchange programs with South Pacific countries were features in the House foreign policy authorization legislation (H.R. 1561).

Few in Congress have urged a halt in U.S. Government-supported agricultural sales abroad in order to assuage Australian concerns, although there is some optimism that the Uruguay Round GATT trade agreement on agricultural trade will reduce U.S. reliance on such sales. Few in Congress have called for increases in U.S. aid and other spending levels in the region, while the Clinton Administration is cutting back U.S. AID, diplomatic, and other support.

Current U.S. Government spending constraints suggest that the main alternative to the current U.S. programs in the region may be a scaled-down effort. Even the modestly funded U.S. programs may be subject to cuts as foreign aid, diplomatic spending, and foreign travel by senior administration and congressional Members alike are viewed with a somewhat more jaundiced eye by an American public concerned with problems at home. The absence of a major regional threat or U.S. policy concern may also make it more difficult for U.S. regional advocates to compete for policymakers' attention amid a rapidly changing world order involving dramatic, high stakes developments elsewhere.

CHRONOLOGY

06/14/96 --- Australia froze military relations with France on account of France's decision to resume nuclear tests in the South Pacific.

06/09/96 --- A British frigate and tanker arrived in Wellington, New Zealand marking the end of an eleven year ban on foreign warships visiting New Zealand as part of its nuclear-free policy.

--- Defense Minister Warren Cooper stated that he is confident that New Zealand troops will be training with U.S. forces by next year in another step to restoring U.S.-New Zealand military relations.

06/07/95 --- New Zealand announced that it will make a firm response if France resumes nuclear testing in the South Pacific area.

03/30/95 --- Papau New Guinea Parliament by a huge majority passed its first vote on constitutional amendments to replace the country's provisional system of government.

03/28/95 --- New Zealand Prime Minister Bolger met with President Clinton, Vice President Gore and other senior administrative officials in a sign of bolstering U.S.-New Zealand relations.

03/20/95 --- Australia and New Zealand committed to contribute 5 million U.S. dollars and 325,000 U.S. dollars respectively to the Korean Peninsula Energy Development Organization (KEDO).

02/03/95 --- Australian trade minister Senator Bob McMullan announced a review of its trading relationship with U.S.

12/10/94 --- Chief of the New Zealand Defense Force, Vice Admiral Sir Sommerford Teagle visited Washington and met with many high level military officials including Chairman of the Joint Chiefs of Staff General John Shalikaskvili and Members of Congress.

11/30/94 --- Australia announced a plan to forge a substantial security partnership with Southeast Asian countries over the next 15 years.

11/14/94 --- Clinton administration officials apologized for laughing at a news briefing in response to a suggestion that Guam should join the Asia Pacific Economic Cooperation (APEC) forum.

10/01/94 --- Palau became an independent state in free association with the U.S.

09/04/94 --- Papua New Guinea government and Bougainville rebel representatives signed a peace agreement.

08/24/94 --- A hurricane reportedly damaged the chemical weapons disposal center at Johnson Island but no traces of escaped poison chemicals were detected.

08/02/94 --- The South Pacific Forum focused on protecting regional fishing and forestry resources. Assistant Secretary Lord attended the post-Forum "dialogue."

06/30/94 -- In a move broadly support in the South Pacific, the United States announced that it would sign the Law of the Sea Treaty.

--- Australia welcomed a U.S. decision to reduce subsidized wheat sales over the next year.

04/11/94 --- U.S. CINPAC Admiral Larson began a visit to New Zealand, the first such visit in a decade.

03/08/94 --- Secretary of State Christopher led a U.S. delegation to Canberra for annual ministerial talks with Australia.

02/18/94 --- The State Department announced the resumption of official contacts with New Zealand.

11/19/93 --- U.S. AID announced it would close its South Pacific office in 1994.

11/17/93 --- New Zealand's National Party formed a government after its narrow victory in the November 6 elections.

11/09/93 --- A referendum in Palau approving the compact with the United States was passed.

10/26/93 --- Press reports said that Britain may withdraw from the South Pacific Commission.

09/14/93 --- Australian Prime Minister Keating held summit talks with President Clinton at the White House.

08/10/93 --- The annual South Pacific Forum summit meeting took place in Nauru.

07/28/93 --- U.S. officials postponed the heretofore annual U.S.-Australian foreign/defense ministers' meeting.

05/10/93 --- A French warship visited New Zealand, the first such visit in nine years.

0313/93 --- Australia's Labor Party won general elections.

02/04/93 -- In Tonga, pro-democracy candidates took a majority of "commoner" seats in the aristocratic/royalty-dominated parliament.

09/01/92 --- Australia and New Zealand normalized military and other relations with Fiji.

08/10/92 --- A South Pacific Forum scientific mission termed as safe the United States chemical weapons disposal system at Johnston Island.

07/15/92 --- The South Pacific Forum annual meeting decided to admit Taiwan as a dialogue partner. China already participates and objected.

04/08/92 --- France suspended its nuclear tests in the Pacific.

12/22/90 -- The U.N. Security Council voted to end the trusteeship covering the Federated States of Micronesia, the Marshall Islands, and the Northern Mariana Islands.

10/27/90 --- President Bush held an unprecedented summit meeting with 11 Pacific Island leaders.

For Additional Reading

Alves, Dora. "New Zealand Faces Quandary." *Defense News*, Sept. 7-13, 1992: 44.

"Australia -- "We're Number 18 and Trying Harder. Survey of Australia." *The Economist*, Apr. 4, 1992: 3-18 (second section).

Colson, David. "U.S. Policy on Tuna-Dolphin Issues." *U.S. Department of State Dispatch*, Aug. 24, 1992: 667-671.

Dorrance, John. *The United States and the Pacific Island*. Praeger, Westport, CT. 1992. 192 p.

Faleomavaega, Eni F. H. "Ensuring Stability in the Pacific." *Christian Science Monitor*, Jan. 11, 1994.

U.S. General Accounting Office. *U.S. Insular Areas: Development strategy and Better Coordination Among U.S. Agencies are Needed*. Report GAO/NSIAD-94-62 February 1994. 32 p.

U.S. Library of Congress. Congressional Research Service. *Pacific Island Nations: Overview of Trends and Problems in the South and West Pacific*, by Luella S. Christopher. [Washington] July 29, 1990. 30 p.
CRS Report 90-396 F

----- *Pacific Island Nations and the United States: Developing a Closer Dialogue*, by Luella S. Christopher. [Washington] Oct. 23, 1990. 35 p.
CRS Report 90-541 F

----- *Political Development of U.S. Insular Areas*, by Andorra Bruno and Garrine Laney. [Washington] May 13, 1992. 39 p.
CRS Report 92-477 GOV

----- *The South Pacific Nuclear Free Zone Treaty*, by Zachary Davis. [Washington] June 25, 1993. 6 p.
CRS Report 93-610 ENR

U.S. ECONOMIC, TRADE, AND FINANCIAL RELATIONS WITH ASIA

James K. Jackson
Specialist in International Trade and Finance
Wayne M. Morrison
Analyst in International Trade and Finance
Economics Division

SUMMARY

The dynamic level of economic growth that has occurred in several Asian nations in recent years has made that region an increasingly important source for international trade and investment flows. This report provides a statistical overview of the following Asian nations: Japan, China, Hong Kong, Taiwan, South Korea, Indonesia, Malaysia, the Philippines, Singapore, Thailand, India, Australia, and New Zealand. The growing importance of this region to the United States in economic terms is reflected in the data.

- In nominal dollar terms using exchange rates, the 1993 combined gross domestic product of the Asian nations ($6,435 billion) was roughly equivalent to U.S. GDP ($6,374 billion). However, the actual purchasing power of Asian GDP was $7,848 billion.
- Per capita GDP in purchasing power parities (PPPs) indicate that U.S. living standards are higher than those of any Asian nation. PPP measurements also show that living standards in several Asian countries are higher than are reflected by data which measures per capita GDP in U.S. dollars using nominal exchange rates.
- Many Asian nations are currently enjoying rapid economic growth relative to the United States, European Union, and other regions of the world. This trend is likely to continue in the near future, making Asia an increasingly important center for trade and investment.
- One factor behind Asia's rapid economic growth has been the high level of savings and investment that exists in many Asian countries. Gross domes-

tic savings and investment as percentages of GDP total 30 percent or more in seven Asian countries.

- Between 1982 and 1992, the total combined trade (exports plus imports) of the major economies of Asia grew by 324 percent. The world share of trade of the major Asian economies grew from 18.9 percent in 1982 to 37.6 percent in 1992.
- The percentage of total U.S. exports going to Asia increased from 25.4 percent in 1983 to 29.6 percent in 1993. U.S. imports from Asia as a percent of total U.S. imports grew from 33.5 percent to 41.7 percent.
- From 1982 to 1992, about 15 percent of U.S. direct investment abroad was invested in Asia. Conversely, Asia accounted for 32 percent (mostly from Japan) of foreign direct investment in the United States.
- direct investment in Asia is concentrated more heavily than in other regions in the petroleum (19 percent) and wholesale trade sectors (16 percent). Manufacturing accounts for 39 percent of investments.

A Statistical Overview

The dynamic economic growth that has occurred in several Asian nations over the past decade has made Asia increasingly important to U.S. economic interests. In recent years, Asia has become one of the world's fastest growing economic regions. From 1985 to 1990, Asia's annual real GDP averaged 4.6 percent. In 1993, Asia's real GDP growth slowed to 2.7 percent, mainly due to Japan's economic recession. However, real GDP growth for the major developing Asia countries (excluding Japan, Australia, and New Zealand) was 7.5 percent. Rapid economic growth in Asia has substantially boosted domestic spending for consumption and domestic investment (such as infrastructure development) in the region, which has generated increased demand for imports. Living standards in many Asian countries have also risen rapidly, increasing the level of demand for certain types of consumer products, high-value manufactures, capital goods, and various types of business services.

Asia's economic development has boosted U.S. trade with the region. Over the past 10 years, U.S. exports to Asia grew by over 163 percent, while imports increased by nearly 180 percent. In 1993, Asia accounted for nearly 30 percent of U.S. exports and close to 42 percent of U.S. imports. U.S. trade with Asia exceeds that with Canada, the European Union, or Latin America.

Many Asian countries are expected to continue to experience healthy rates of economic growth (relative to other regions) in the years ahead, which means that Asia (especially developing Asia) will likely continue to grow in importance as a destination for U.S. exports, both in terms of total exports and as a percentage of overall U.S. exports.

U.S. direct investment in the region remains small relative to that in Europe and Latin America. About 32 percent of foreign direct investment in the United States over the past 10 years came from Asia, mostly from Japan.

The purpose of this report is to provide a statistical overview of U.S. economic, trade and investment relations with the major economic nations of Asia, including Japan, China, Hong Kong, Taiwan, South Korea, Singapore, Malaysia, the Philippines, Indonesia, Thailand, India, New Zealand, and Australia.[1] All references to Asia, hereafter (unless otherwise noted) refer to these nations. Data are presented with bulleted summary statements describing the significance and trends of U.S. economic relations with Asia.

ECONOMIC DATA[2]

GROSS DOMESTIC PRODUCT

Gross domestic product (GDP) provides a broad economic measurement of the value of a nation's domestically produced goods and services. Per capita GDP is a commonly used measurement to make international comparisons of living standards.

In order to compare U.S. GDP with other nations, a standard of measurement (currency) is needed, such as U.S. dollars. One method of converting foreign data into U.S. dollars is to use nominal exchange rates. However, such measurements may be misleading because exchange rates fluctuate widely from year to year, and the magnitude of those fluctuations bears little correlation with changes in real GDP. In addition, such measurements do not adequately reflect differences in prices that exist across nations. Hence, a measurement of GDP is needed which factors in the cost of living (prices) and eliminates the distorting effects of volatile exchange rates.

Purchasing power parities (PPPs) are rates of currency conversion that equalize the purchasing power of different currencies. That is, they indicate the purchasing power one currency would have to purchase a similar level of goods and services in another country. PPPs are calculated by making international comparisons of prices for various goods and services. This involves choosing a "basket of goods and services" that is considered to be representative of typical consumer purchases of each country, then making measurements of the amount of goods and services each currency (expressed in dollars, for example) would be able to purchase. The resulting PPP measurements provide a more accurate method for making international comparisons of GDP since they more precisely

---

[1] Although Australia and New Zealand are not technically part of Asia, they are often classified by various organizations as Asian countries (or part of the Asia-Pacific Rim area) for the purpose of reporting trade and investment data.

[2] Prepared by Wayne M. Morrison, Analyst in International Trade and Finance.

reflect the actual material *purchasing power* of the GDP of various nations in their home markets relative to U.S. GDP.

The difference in using nominal exchange rates as opposed to using PPPs to measure GDP in dollars is illustrated in the following example. Japan's 1993 GDP expressed in nominal exchange rate dollars was $4,243 billion. However, because prices for domestic goods and services are generally higher in Japan than the United States, the actual purchasing power of Japan's GDP was $2,534 billion.[3]

Table 1 provides data on GDP and per capita GDP using nominal exchange rates and PPPs for the Asian nations, the United States, and other regions of the world.

- In nominal dollar terms using exchange rates, the 1993 combined GDP of the Asian nations ($6,435 billion) was roughly equivalent to U.S. GDP ($6,374 billion) an that of the EU ($6,374 billion). However, the actual purchasing power of combined Asian GDP was $7,848 billion, 23 percent higher than that of the United States or the EU.
- PPP data indicate that several developing Asian countries have much higher GDPs than is reflected by data which uses nominal exchange rates. For example, China's 1993 GDP using nominal exchange rates was $520 billion. However, expressed in PPPs, China's GDP was $1,847 billion. This measurement would make China the world's third largest economy after the United States and Japan.
- Japan's 1993 per capita GDP in nominal exchange rate dollars was $34,181, 38.6 percent higher than that of the United States ($24,664). However, in terms of actual *purchasing power*, Japan's per capita GDP (PPPs) was actually worth $20,335. This indicates that U.S. per capita GDP (PPPs) is actually 21.2 percent higher than Japan's, and is greater than that of any other Asian country.
- Hong Kong maintains the highest living standards (per capita GDP in PPPs) among the Asian nations, followed by Japan, Singapore, Australia, New Zealand, and Taiwan.
- PPP data indicate that living standards in several developing Asian countries are much higher than reflected by per capita GDP using exchange rates. For example, in 1993, the actual purchasing power of India's $292 per capita (GDP (exchange rate U.S. dollars) was $1,196 (PPPs).

---

[3] DRI/McGraw-Hill estimates that, on average, prices in Japan are 68 percent greater than in the United States.

TABLE 1. Gross Domestic Product and Per Capita GDP in Nominal U.S. Exchange Rate Dollars and Purchasing Power Parities (PPP) for Asia, the United States and the EU: 1993

	Gross Domestic Product ($ Billions)		Per Capita GDP ($)	
	Nominal Exchange Rates	Purchasing Power Parities	Nominal Exchange Rates	Purchasing Power Parities
Hong Kong	$109	$122	$18,570	$20,969
Japan	4,259	2,534	34,181	20,335
Singapore	50	52	17,746	18,410
Australia	278	309	15,861	17,660
New Zealand	43	49	12,386	14,945
Taiwan	221	402	10,521	10,154
South Korea	324	402	7,345	9,124
Malaysia	64	172	3,335	8,951
Thailand	117	342	1,971	5,761
Indonesia	139	617	716	3,171
Philippines	55	152	840	2,306
China	520	1,847	436	1,550
India	256	1,046	292	1,196
Total Selected Asia	6,435	7,848	2,452	2,996
Developing Asia*	1,854	5,011	748	2,003
United States	6,374	6,374	24,664	24,664
European Union	6,374	5,795	18,369	16,754

***Excluded Japan, Australia, and New Zealand.**

Source: DRI\McGraw Hill, *World Markets Country Summaries*, First Quarter 1994, various pages.

ECONOMIC GROWTH

As indicated in table 2, Asia over the past years has become one of the world's most dynamic regions for economic growth.

- Average annual real GDP growth in Asia from 1980-1985 and 1985-1990 was 3.8 percent and 4.6 percent, respectively. These rates of growth were significantly faster than those in the United States, the EU, and most other regions of the world.
- In 1993, Japan's real GDP grew by only 0.2 over the previous year. The EU's real GDP decreased by 0.4 percent. However, the developing Asian nations (excluding Japan, Australia, and New Zealand) grew by 7.5 percent.

- Asia's annual GDP is projected to increase by 4.6 percent in 1994 and 3.5 percent in 1995. However the developing Asian nations are projected to grow even faster: 6.8 percent in 1994 and 6.3 percent in 1995. This indicates that developing Asia is likely to be the world's fastest growing economic region in the near future.

TABLE 2. Annual Average GDP Growth for Asia and Selective Regions: 1980-2000, Actual and Projected (%)

	Actual		Projected			
	1980-1985 Average Annual Rate	1985-1990 Average Annual Rate	1993	1994	1995	1995-2000 Average Annual Rate
Japan	3.8%	4.6%	0.2%	0.3%	3.6%	2.8%
China	10.0	6.0	13.0	10.3	7.9	8.0
Taiwan	6.7	8.7	6.7	6.5	6.5	6.3
South Korea	8.4	10.2	4.3	6.5	7.1	6.5
Indonesia	5.0	6.2	6.6	6.8	7.0	6.2
Malaysia	5.1	6.8	7.2	6.8	6.8	6.5
Philippines	-1.3	4.6	1.5	3.0	4.4	5.5
Singapore	6.2	7.9	6.2	5.7	5.8	4.4
Thailand	5.6	9.9	7.2	7.9	7.1	6.1
India	5.4	6.1	5.1	5.6	5.7	5.5
Australia	3.3	3.0	0.2	0.3	3.6	2.8
New Zealand	3.0	0.6	2.7	2.7	2.9	3.1
Total Asia	3.8	4.6	2.7	4.6	3.5	4.2
Developing Asia[a]	6.2	6.9	6.7	6.8	6.3	5.9
United States	2.5	2.7	2.9	3.6	1.9	2.5
European Union	1.5	3.1	-0.4	1.0	2.5	3.0
Non-EU Europe[b]	2.1	3.0	0.2	1.6	2.5	2.8
Latin America[c]	0.7	1.5	3.9	4.6	4.6	5.0
Middle East & Africa[d]	2.4	0.9	4.9	3.3	2.8	4.1

[a] Excludes Japan, Australia, and New Zealand.

[b] Includes Austria, Finland, Norway, Sweden, Switzerland, and Turkey.

[c] Includes Argentina, Brazil, Chile, Columbia, Ecuador, Mexico, Peru, and Venezuela.

[d] Includes Algeria, Egypt, Iran, Kuwait, Nigeria, and Saudi Arabia

Source: DRI\McGraw Hill, *World Markets Executive Overview*, First Quarter 1994, p. 51.

SAVINGS AND INVESTMENT

One factor that has been attributed to the sharp rate of economic growth that has occurred in several Asian countries has been the high rate of savings and investment in such countries. A high rate of domestic savings enables nations to finance a high level of domestic investment, which in turn can generate high rates of economic growth (due mainly to increases in productivity resulting from investment). In addition, a high savings rate can enable a country to finance its own domestic investment without having to borrow capital from abroad. Table 3 indicates gross domestic savings and investment as percentages of GDP. These data indicate that savings and investment rates in most Asian countries are far above the world average and those of the United States. Gross domestic savings and investment as percentages of GDP total or exceed 30 percent in seven Asian countries.

TABLE 3. Gross Domestic Savings and Investment as a Percentage of GDP for the World, the United States and Selected Asian Nations: 1992

	Gross Domestic Savings as a % of GDP	Gross Domestic Investment as a % of GDP
World	22%	22%
United States	15	16
Japan	34	31
China	38	37
Taiwan	28	24
South Korea	35	40
Indonesia	36	35
Malaysia	30	36
Philippines	15	22
Singapore	46	40
Thailand	34	36
India	22	24
Australia	19	20
New Zealand	20	19

Sources: World Bank, *World Development Report 1994;* and Asian Development Bank, *Asian Development Outlook 1992.*

TRADE[4]

WORLD TRADE RANKINGS FOR ASIAN COUNTRIES

Table 4 provides data on total trade (exports plus imports) for the United States and Asian countries for 1982 and 1992. These data indicate that several Asian countries have experienced rapid growth in trade over the past ten years.

TABLE 4. Asian Trade: Total Trade, Percentage of World Trade, and Trade Rankings, 1982 and 1992 ($ Billions)

	1982			1992			
	Total Trade	Percent of World Trade	World Ranking	Total Trade	World Ranking	Percent of World Trade	1982/1992 % Increase in Trade
Asia	**$668**	**18.9%**	--	**$1,819**	--	**24.1%**	**172%**
Japan	270	7.6	3	572	3	7.6	112
New Zealand	11	0.3	53	19	50	0.3	68
Australia	49	1.4	16	87	22	1.2	79
Developing Asia	338	9.6	--	1,140	--	15.1	237
Hong Kong	44	1.3	18	243	10	3.2	449
China	41	1.2	21	168	11	2.2	311
S. Korea	46	1.3	17	156	13	2.1	239
Taiwan	42	1.2	19	154	14	2.0	267
Singapore	49	1.4	15	134	15	1.8	173
Malaysia	25	0.7	34	81	23	1.1	229
Thailand	16	0.4	45	73	25	1.0	372
Indonesia	39	1.1	22	61	26	0.8	57
India	24	0.7	35	44	34	0.6	84
Philippines	13	0.4	50	27	44	0.4	99
United States	467	13.2	1	1,000	1	13.2	114
World	3,535	100	--	7,549	--	100	114

Total trade is exports plus imports (c.i.f. basis)

Rankings and calculations performed by CRS.

Source: International Monetary Fund, *Direction of Trade Statistics.*

Data obtained by CRS using Tradenet.

[4]Prepared by Wayne M. Morrison, Analyst in International Trade and Finance.

- Between 1982 and 1992 Asian trade grew from $668 billion to $1,819 billion, a 172 percent increase.
- Asia's share of world trade rose from 18.9 percent in 1982 to 24.1 percent in 1992.
- The U.S. and Japanese share of world trade over the past 10 years remained constant at 13.2 percent and 7.6 percent, respectively. However the share of trade for the developing Asian economies rose from 9.6 percent in 1982 to 15.1 percent in 1992. Trade by the developing Asian countries grew by 237 percent.

U.S. Trade With Asia Compared With Other Regions

Asia has become an increasingly important destination for U.S. exports and source for U.S. imports, as indicated in tables 5 and 6.

- Asia constitutes the largest regional destination for U.S. exports and the largest source of U.S. imports.
- From 1983 to 1993, U.S. exports to Asia rose from $52.3 billion to $137.7 billion, an increase of $85.4 billion or 163.2 percent.
- exports to Asia as a percentage of total U.S. exports rose from 25.4 percent in 1983 to 29.6 percent in 1993.
- imports from Asia also grew sharply relative to other regions of the world, rising from $86.5 billion in 1983 to $241.9 billion in 1993, an increase of $155.4 billion of 179.6 percent.
- imports from Asia as a percent of total imports rose from 33.5 percent in 1983 to 41.7 percent in 1993.

TABLE 5. U.S. Exports to Asia and Other Regions of the World: 1983 and 1993 ($ Millions)

	1983		1993		
	U.S. Exports	As a % of Total U.S. Exports	U.S. Exports	As a % of Total U.S. Exports	1983/1993 % Growth in U.S. Exports
World	$205,639	100.0%	$464,858	100.0%	126.1%
Asia	**52,312**	**25.4**	**137,704**	**29.6**	**163.2**
Canada	42,971	20.9	100,190	21.6	133.2

Table 5 (Continued)

Africa	7,666	3.7	9,286	2.0	21.1
Latin America	25,532	12.4	78,477	16.9	207.4
European Union	47,652	23.2	96,957	20.9	103.5
Other Western Europe	7,426	3.6	16,698	3.6	124.9
Former USSR and Eastern Europe	2,887	1.4	6,069	1.3	110.2
Middle East	11,827	5.8	16,841	3.6	42.4
All Other	7,346	3.6	2,636	0.6	-64.1

Source: U.S. Department of Commerce. Calculations made by CRS.

TABLE 6. U.S. Imports from Asia and Other Regions of the World: 1983 and 1993 ($ Millions)

	1983		1993		
	U.S. Imports	As a % of Total U.S. Imports	U.S. Imports	As a % of Total U.S. Imports	1983/1993 % Growth in U.S. Imports
World	$258,050	100.0%	$580,469	100.0%	124.9%
Asia	**86,501**	**33.5**	**241,883**	**41.7**	**179.6**
Canada	52,130	20.2	110,921	19.1	112.8
Africa	14,420	5.6	14,786	2.5	2.5
Latin America	41,725	16.2	74,395	12.8	78.3
European Union	45,712	17.7	98,007	16.9	114.4
Other Western Europe	8,176	3.2	17,599	3.0	115.3
Former USSR and Eastern Europe	1,357	0.5	3,523	0.6	159.6
Middle East	7,134	2.8	15,396	2.7	115.8
All Other	895	0.3	3,959	0.7	342.3

Source: U.S. Department of Commerce. Calculations made by CRS.

U.S.-ASIAN TRADE BY COUNTRY

Tables 7, 8, and 9 provide data on U.S. trade with each Asian country for 1983 and 1993.

- In 1993, eight of the top 20 destinations for U.S. exports were Asian countries. Nine of the top 20 sources of U.S. imports were Asian nations.

- The top three Asian destinations for U.S. exports in 1993 were Japan, Taiwan, and South Korea.
- The U.S. export ranking of 10 of the 13 Asian countries surveyed increased. For example, Hong Kong went from being the United States' 19th largest export market in 1983 to the 11th largest in 1993. Japan's ranking for U.S. exports remained unchanged, while the export rankings for the two remaining Asian countries decreased.
- The top three Asian sources of U.S. imports in 1993 were Japan, Taiwan, and China.
- The U.S. import ranking of seven Asian countries increased during this period. For example, China went from being the 23rd largest source of U.S. imports in 1983 to the 4th largest in 1993. Two Asian country import rankings remained unchanged, while four others fell.
- The U.S. trade deficit with Asia rose sharply, from $34.2 billion in 1983 to $104.2 billion in 1993, a 204.7 percent increase.

TABLE 7. U.S. Exports to Asian Nations for 1983 and 1993: Totals, Rankings, and % Change ($ Millions)

	1983		1993		
	Exports	Rank for U.S. Exports	Exports	Rank for U.S. Exports	1983/1993 % Change in Exports
Japan	$21,600	2	$47,949	2	122.0%
Taiwan	4,401	12	16,250	6	269.2
Korea South	5,710	10	14,776	7	158.8
Singapore	3,686	15	11,676	10	216.8
Hong Kong	2,563	19	9,873	11	285.2
China	2,173	21	8,767	13	303.5
Australia	3,916	13	8,272	14	111.2
Malaysia	1,678	28	6,064	18	261.4
Thailand	906	35	3,768	24	315.9
Philippines	1,793	26	3,529	25	96.8
Indonesia	1,446	31	2,770	29	91.6
India	1,827	25	2,761	31	51.1
New Zealand	613	46	1,247	41	103.4
Total Selected Asia	52,312	--	137,704	--	163.2

Countries listed in order of U.S. export rank in 1993.
Source: U.S. Department of Commerce.

- Japan and China accounted for a significant share of the U.S. trade deficit with Asia in 1993.
- The U.S. trade deficit with China rose from $71 million in 1983 to $22.8 billion in 1993. The U.S. trade deficit with Japan over this period rose from $19.6 billion to $59.3 billion.
- In 1993, the United States maintained trade surpluses with Australia, Hong Kong, and New Zealand.

TABLE 8. U.S. Imports From Asian Nations for 1983 and 1993: Totals, Rankings, and % Change ($ Millions)

	1983		1993		
	Imports	Rank for U.S. Exports	Imports	Rank for U.S. Exports	1983/1993 % Change
Japan	$41,183	2	$107,268	2	160.5%
China	2,244	23	31,535	4	1,305.3
Taiwan	11,204	6	25,105	6	124.1
Korea South	7,148	7	17,123	8	139.5
Singapore	2,868	18	12,796	11	346.2
Malaysia	2,124	26	10,568	12	397.6
Hong Kong	6,394	8	9,558	13	49.5
Thailand	967	40	8,542	14	783.4
Indonesia	5,285	11	5,439	20	2.9
Philippines	2,001	28	4,895	23	144.6
India	2,191	25	4,551	24	107.7
Australia	2,222	24	3,294	27	48.2
New Zealand	730	45	1,208	44	65.5
Total Selected Asia	86,501	--	241,883	--	179.6

Countries listed in order of U.S. import rank in 1993.
Source: U.S. Department of Commerce.

TABLE 9. U.S. Trade Balances with Asian Countries: 1983 and 1993 ($ Millions)

	1983	1993
Japan	-19,583	-59,318
China	-71	-22,768
Taiwan	-6,803	-8,855
Korea, South	-1,438	-2,347
Singapore	818	-1,121
Malaysia	-446	-4,504
Hong Kong	-3,831	315
Thailand	-61	-4,773
Indonesia	-3,838	-2,669
Philippines	-208	-1,366
India	-364	-1,790
Australia	1,694	4,978
New Zealand	-117	39
Selected Partner Countries	-34,249	-104,179

Source: U.S. Department of Commerce.

ASIAN TRADE WITH SELECTED WORLD REGIONS

Table 10 indicates the combined level of trade (exports plus imports) by the Asian countries with various regions of the world for 1982 and 1992.

- Asia's trade with the United States as a share of its total trade fell slightly, 20.3 percent in 1982 to 20.1 percent in 1992.
- Asia's trade with the Middle East as a share of its total trade fell sharply, from 14.1 percent in 1982 to 5.1 percent in 1992, due mainly to falling petroleum prices.
- The share of Asian trade with the developing Asian countries grew from 24.8 percent in 1982 to 34.9 percent in 1992. Japan's share of Asia's trade fell slightly over this period from 11.9 percent to 11.8 percent, indicating that most of the increase in trade by the Asian countries with developing Asia has been between the developing Asian countries.

TABLE 10. Asian Trade with Various Countries and Regions: 1982 and 1992
($ Billions and % of Total Trade)

	1983		1993	
Asian Trade Partner	Total Asian Trade	% of Total Asian Trade	Total Asian Trade	% of Total Asian Trade
World	$665.9	100%	$1,820.0	100%
Industrial Countries	346.3	52.0	973.4	53.5
United States	135.1	20.3	365.8	20.1
Japan	79.2	11.9	214.0	11.8
European Union	74.1	11.1	266.7	14.7
Other Industrial	57.9	8.7	126.9	7.0
Developing Countries	302.1	45.4	793.2	43.6
Europe	4.3	0.6	10.4	0.6
Western Hemisphere	22.9	3.4	44.6	2.5
Middle East	94.1	14.1	92.8	5.1
Asia*	165.4	24.8	634.4	34.9
Africa	15.5	2.3	15.5	0.9
Former USSR, Eastern Europe, and Other	14.6	2.2	14.6	0.9

* Includes all the developing countries of Asia (based on IMF regional definitions).

Total trade is exports plus imports (c.i.f. basis).

Source: International Monetary Fund, *Direction of Trade Statistics*. Data obtained by CRS using Tradenet.

U.S. Financial and Investment Relations with Asia[5]

The following tables provide data on direct investment flows between the United States and Asia, the overall level, or position of direct investment, and the annual amounts of bilateral financial flows reported in the U.S. balance of payments. The United States defines direct investment as the ownership or control, directly or indirectly, by a single person (individual, branch, partnership, associated group, association, estate, trust, corporation, or any government) of 10 percent of more of the voting securities of an incorporated business enterprise or the equivalent interest in an unincorporated business enterprise.[6]

[5]Prepared by James K. Jackson, Specialist in International Trade and Finance.

[6]15 CFR § 806.15(a)(1).

TABLE 11. U.S. Direct Investment Abroad - Capital Outflows, 1982-1992
($ Millions)

	1982	1983	1984	1985	1986	1987	1988	1989	1990	1991	1992
Total	3,835	6,686	11,649	12,724	17,706	28,980	17,871	37,604	27,705	32,098	37,122
Canada	-339	878	3,260	76	2,491	6,099	2,653	1,268	3,471	1,164	3,257
Europe	106	5,122	5,578	7,573	7,292	11,397	7,854	23,679	8,544	18,928	13,409
France	-103	155	177	944	394	1,008	1,663	1,584	1,053	2,092	2,836
Germany	-73	632	357	213	1,070	644	-1,873	2,522	1,464	6,133	1,571
Netherlands	-16	134	-118	569	3,304	2,000	1,391	3,112	-2,401	1,555	-2,355
Spain	85	198	-23	247	444	436	492	979	391	-16	1,359
Switzerland	241	1,454	779	367	220	1,652	-1,083	1,269	5,284	897	2,997
United Kingdom	-114	1,385	3,052	3,147	2,259	2,559	4,170	11,825	-629	3,359	3,545
Latin America	878	-3,002	774	4,203	7,287	8,132	6,042	9,094	9,510	6,870	13,673
Africa	683	23	320	-50	-161	301	-376	-554	-504	104	-1,045
Middle East	282	1,258	596	-74	73	237	-270	-473	563	660	1,085
Asia	1,523	2,234	1,638	675	1,390	3,047	2,584	4,375	6,223	4,390	6,560
Australia	41	250	165	299	-46	981	687	1,997	678	1,071	1,335
China	24	51	100	172	-98	112	103	100	32	54	44
Hong Kong	55	341	335	18	691	280	567	465	265	420	1,856
India	28	19	-3	43	51	61	53	(D)	(D)	73	52
Indonesia	1,041	474	932	220	37	-322	-138	-65	659	608	656
Japan	226	999	-245	333	343	1160	1036	299	844	244	867
Korea, Rep.	(D)	-122	124	42	58	156	141	332	312	194	-140
Malaysia	(D)	-88	-128	36	-91	-59	133	50	222	185	55
New Zealand	54	-36	-31	46	33	89	92	162	1962	-243	138
Philippines	61	129	-22	-242	42	-6	80	49	177	-27	-17
Singapore	-33	83	199	-79	193	179	-105	165	481	1127	1097
Taiwan	68	70	99	2	80	345	191	177	209	429	154
Thailand	50	115	213	-43	-1	183	-153	384	315	242	367

Note: (D) indicates that data have been suppressed by the Department of Commerce to avoid the disclosure of individual companies; an (*) indicates that values are less than $500,000.

Source: *Survey of Current Business*, various issues.

Table 11 shows the annual amounts of U.S. direct investment abroad to major regions of the world from 1982 to 1992. Figure 1 shows the distribution of U.S. direct investment capital outflows by share by major region.

- During the first half of the 1980s, U.S. direct investment abroad was moderate, reflecting the favorable investment climate in the United States. This trend was changed in the last half of the 1980s and into the 1990s, as U.S. firms have emerged as the largest foreign direct investors.
- During the 1982-1992 period, nearly half of all U.S. direct investment abroad was invested in Europe.
- About 15 percent of U.S. direct investment abroad was invested in Asia, the third most preferred region after Europe and Latin America.

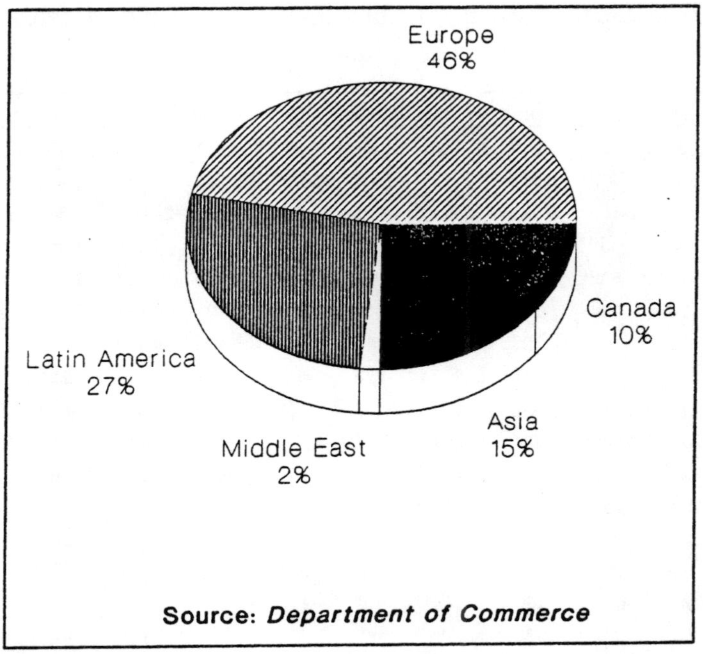

FIGURE 1. U.S. Direct Investment Abroad Share by Region
Total Capital Outflows, 1982-1992 (percent)

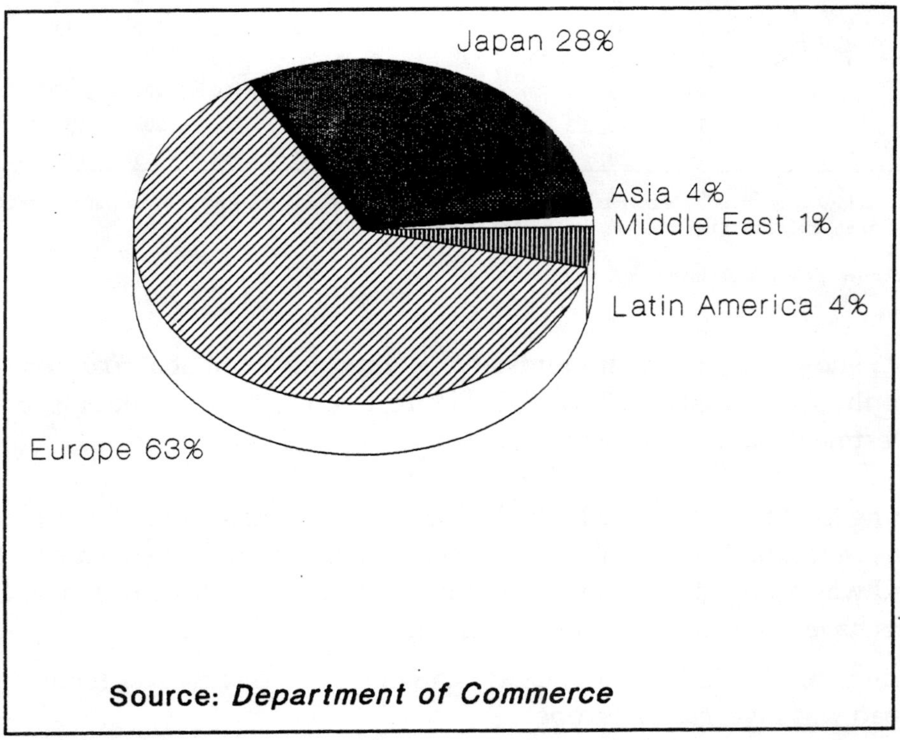

FIGURE 2. Foreign Direct Investment in the United States
Share by Region, Total Capital Inflows 1982-1992 (percent)

TABLE 12. Foreign Direct Investment in the United States - Capital Inflows, 1982-1992 ($ Millions)

	1982	1983	1984	1985	1986	1987	1988	1989	1990	1991	1992
Total	13,792	11,946	25,359	19,022	34,091	41,977	58,571	69,010	48,422	25,446	3,388
Canada	-1,331	215	3,294	911	2,547	959	1,852	1,793	1,821	2,383	-2,144
Europe	10,458	9,134	14,686	12,794	21,730	34,974	31,852	43,046	21,549	13,047	8
France	-195	-201	774	30	1,017	2,551	3,122	2,744	5,987	4,462	-468
Germany	419	1,007	1,291	2,292	1,982	2,403	2,245	3,738	585	2,167	1,389
Netherlands	3,434	2,778	3,520	2,776	4,374	7,871	6,137	7,323	7,163	1,006	-1,491
Sweden	48	358	216	236	1,395	744	-95	587	443	274	1,381
Switzerland	934	962	1,035	2,722	1,414	2,582	831	5,184	-633	1,490	528
United Kingdom	5,321	3,727	6,882	4,665	10,827	18,562	19,617	18,939	4,519	4,382	-2,608
Latin America	1,629	474	615	719	-332	-1,453	2,944	4,069	5,199	-1,513	841
Africa	NA	NA	NA	NA	NA	NA	-41	55	-8	90	-6
Middle East	798	16	791	-370	-68	193	1,376	900	-613	465	4
Asia	2,323	2,053	5,874	4,717	10,416	7,351	20,587	19,147	20,474	10,975	4,685
Australia	150	210	1,188	1,209	2,606	907	2,741	-81	1,279	-200	663
China	(D)	(D)	14	1	2	1	-61	98	37	4	-1
Hong Kong	52	82	306	2	41	187	88	388	259	339	5
India	1	5	4	3	-1	-7	-2	5	3	-15	-3
Indonesia	-3	2	18	33	-11	3	26	17	-13	2	36
Japan	1,977	1,653	4,374	3,394	7,268	6,181	17,205	18,653	18,754	10,660	3,960
Korea, Rep.	54	-1	-24	-3	474	-181	353	-821	-698	333	46
Malaysia	-6	8	(*)	-5	23	-33	52	(*)	19	-14	13
New Zealand	-3	2	-46	20	29	91	-70	-47	56	(*)	-23
Philippines	25	14	5	-3	-5	9	5	6	-5	-28	8
Singapore	71	89	23	34	-73	189	119	471	370	-419	-22
Taiwan	5	-11	1	37	71	-38	131	421	356	312	7
Thailand	(*)	(*)	11	-5	-8	42	-6	28	55	-11	2

Note: (D) indicates that data have been suppressed by the Department of Commerce to avoid the disclosure of individual companies; an (*) indicates that values are less than $500,000.

Source: *Survey of Current Business*, various issues.

Table 12 shows the capital inflows associated with foreign direct investment in the United States during the 1982-1992 period.

- European firms, as a group, continue to be the major foreign direct investors in the United States.
- Japanese firms became major foreign direct investors in the United States during the 1980s, rising from the fifth to the second largest investors, following United Kingdom investors.
- Other Asian (non-Japanese) investors account for 4 percent of the direct investment capital inflows during the 1982-1992 period, slightly ahead of Latin American investors.

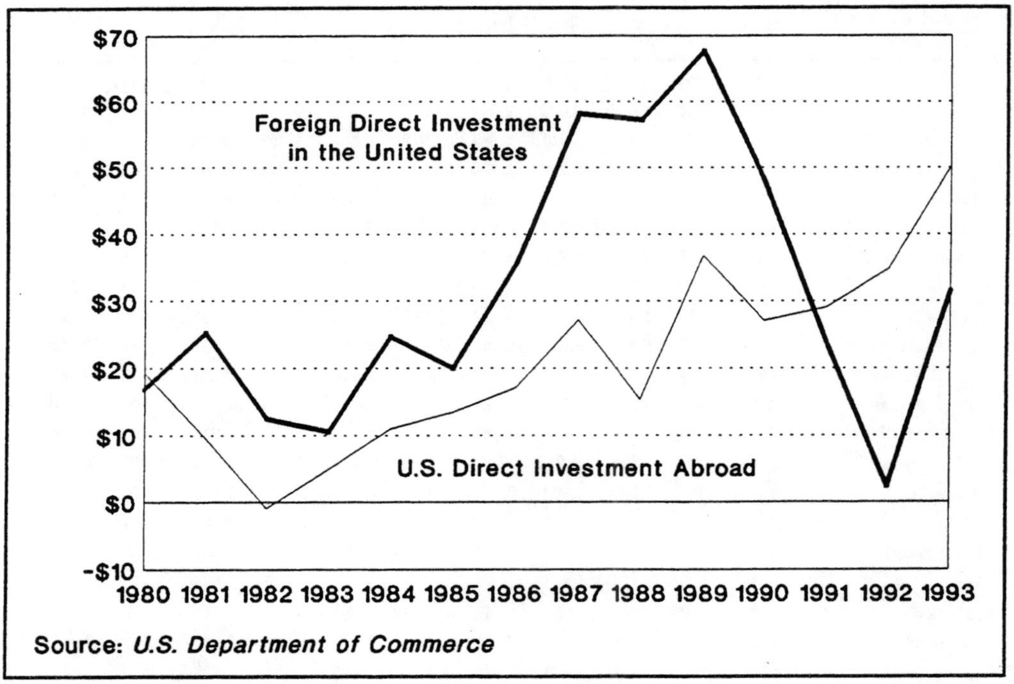

FIGURE 3. U.S. Direct Investment Flows
(in Billions of U.S. Dollars)

Figure 3 shows direct investment flows into and out of the United States from 1980 to 1993. The 1993 data are preliminary balance of payments data and subject to revision by the Department of Commerce.

- That foreign direct investment inflows generally increased during the 1980s and then dropped off between 1989 and 1992.
- According to recent balance of payments data, foreign direct inflows picked up again in 1993.
- The data also show that flows of U.S. direct investment abroad have generally increased since 1982, when U.S. firms pulled capital out of their affiliates abroad to invest in their parent firms in the United States.

TABLE 13. U.S. Direct Investment Position Abroad on a Historical-Cost Basis, 1992 ($ Millions)

	All industries	Petroleum	Manufacturing	Wholesale trade	Banking	Finance (except banking), insurance, and real estate	Services	Other industries
Total	486,670	55,207	187,276	51,140	23,468	129,546	15,789	24,245
Canada	68,432	7,945	33,306	5,567	888	12,938	2,330	5,457
Europe	239,389	23,289	93,733	29,685	9,488	67,225	10,327	5,642
Latin America	88,860	4,559	26,727	3,342	7,731	40,537	1,066	4,898
Africa	3,518	1,523	960	103	133	467	84	248
Middle East	5,814	1,791	1,742	275	141	1,418	242	205
Asia	78,163	14,893	30,808	12,169	5,086	6,960	1,739	6,508
Australia	16,697	2,691	6,631	1,424	1,011	1,523	686	2,731
China	469	91	260	94	(*)	1	(D)	(D)
Hong Kong	8,544	385	2,243	2,914	932	1,291	349	430
India	479	(D)	201	23	233	(D)	15	(*)
Indonesia	4,278	3,686	138	46	(D)	13	(D)	294
Japan	26,213	4,768	11,920	5,424	200	2,707	584	609
Korea, Rep.	2,779	67	1,140	276	1,122	165	25	-17
Malaysia	1,714	513	747	106	91	233	1	23
New Zealand	3,008	397	417	82	(D)	195	(D)	1,925
Philippines	1,565	(D)	1,021	126	340	(D)	(D)	64
Singapore	6,631	1,213	3,460	892	365	369	276	55
Taiwan	2,870	(D)	1,806	469	327	158	59	(D)
Thailand	2,459	774	783	254	230	(D)	47	(D)

Note: (*) indicates that values are less than $500,000. (D) indicates that data have been suppressed by the Department of Commerce to avoid disclosing data of individual companies.

Source: *Survey of Current Business*, July 1993. p. 101.

Table 13 shows the U.S. direct investment position abroad for 1992, the most recent year for which data are available. The position is the total, or the cumulative, amount of investment U.S. firms have made abroad. These data represent the historical cost, or the book value of the investments at the time the investments were made. Most analysts believe the historical cost undervalues U.S. direct investments abroad because it does not account for the effects of inflation on asset values or of growth in the size and value of the foreign affiliates. The Department of Commerce estimates that at market value, U.S. direct investment abroad totals $776 billion, compared with $487 billion at book value. The direct investment position data indicate that:

- Half of all U.S. direct investments abroad are in Europe; eighteen percent are in Latin America; and 16 percent are in Asia.
- Nearly 40 percent of total U.S. direct investment abroad is in the manufacturing sector; 27 percent is in finance; 11 percent is in petroleum; and 10 percent is in wholesale trade. The rest of U.S. direct investments is in the banking and services sectors, and in other industries.
- U.S. direct investment in Asia is concentrated more heavily than in other regions in the petroleum (19 percent) and wholesale trade sectors (16 percent). Manufacturing accounts for 39 percent of investments.

TABLE 14. Foreign Direct Investment Position in the United States on a Historical Cost Basis, 1992
($ Million)

	All industries	Petroleum	Manufacturing	Wholesale trade	Banking	Finance, except banking	Insurance	Real estate	Other industries
Total	419,526	38,545	159,492	66,203	22,848	10,962	34,030	35,244	52,202
Canada	38,997	1,342	17,313	2,307	2,095	1,803	3,691	4,816	5,631
Europe	248,461	30,015	113,595	27,092	9,877	-716	27,230	10,931	30,437
Latin America	18,895	2,334	5,784	2,906	1843	17	2294	2025	1693
Africa	635	(D)	(D)	(D)	-3	(D)	(*)	-56	(D)
Middle East	4,813	(D)	(D)	(D)	672	(D)	2	1,165	(D)
Asia	107,725	2,871	22,461	33,409	8,364	9,241	814	16,363	14,201
Australia	7,140	2,892	1,826	(D)	-290	(D)	165	352	1,941
Hong Kong	1,714	-2	184	988	241	250	2	169	-119
Japan	96,743	-13	19,149	31,761	7,882	9,760	587	15,429	12,190
Korea, Rep.	-496	-2	76	(D)	118	(D)	(D)	11	(D)
Malaysia	54	(*)	22	49	-18	(*)	(*)	2	(*)
New Zealand	108	(*)	-10	125	2	-27	(D)	28	(D)
Philippines	59	(*)	5	-1	38	(*)	(D)	-2	(D)
Singapore	847	(*)	405	31	32	55	(*)	316	9
Taiwan	1,154	(*)	692	97	188	(D)	(D)	23	80

Note: (*) indicates that values are less than $500,000. (D) indicates that data have been suppressed by the Department of Commerce to avoid disclosing data of individual companies.

Source: *Survey of Current Business*, July 1993.

Table 14 shows the foreign direct investment position in the United States. These data are also on a historical costs basis. Since most foreign investments in the United States were made in the 1980s, however, they are not affected as much by the effects of inflation or growth as is U.S. direct investment abroad. The data suggest the following conclusions:

- Nearly 40 percent of foreign direct investment in the United States is in the manufacturing sector (about the same proportion as U.S. direct investment abroad); 16 percent is in wholesale trade. Foreign direct investment in petroleum, real estate, and insurance each comprise about 8 percent of the total; the rest is in banking, finance, and other industries.
- Direct investment from Asia is dominated by investments from Japan. These investments are more concentrated in wholesale trade (31 percent) than in manufacturing (21 percent); another 15 percent of investments is in real estate.

Tables 15, 16 and 17 provide the broad measures of U.S. economic transactions with Asia, including trade in goods and services and capital account transactions. Where "Asia" is indicated in the table, it refers to all Asian countries, except Japan, but includes Africa as well. Since U.S. trade and financial relations with Africa are small compared with Asia, the addition of these countries is unlikely to have a major effect on the overall flows between the United States and Asia. Since U.S. transactions with Japan dominate U.S. trade and financial transactions with Asia, transactions with Asia (table 16) and Japan (table 17) are presented separately.

TABLE 15. U.S. International Transactions: Asia* and Japan
($Billions)

	1983	1984	1985	1986	1987	1988	1989	1990	1991	1992	1993
Exports of goods, services, and income	107.1	111.3	104.1	114.7	129.2	166.1	189.2	208.2	219.9	227.8	236.5
Merchandise exports, adjusted	66.6	68.0	63.3	68.6	77.1	105.2	120.0	127.0	137.5	144.7	152.1
Services receipts	24.7	25.3	25.7	30.8	33.6	36.3	41.2	48.8	56.0	61.3	64.0
Royalties and license fees receipts	1.2	1.4	1.5	1.9	2.5	3.2	3.7	4.2	4.7	5.1	5.8
Income receipts on U.S. assets abroad	15.8	18.0	15.1	15.3	18.4	24.7	28.0	32.5	26.4	21.8	20.4
Direct investment receipts	6.1	6.8	5.2	5.0	7.3	8.4	8.4	9.7	11.0	11.4	11.6
Other private receipts	7.2	8.4	7.0	7.0	8.3	12.2	17.7	17.6	12.7	8.3	7.0
Imports of goods, services, and income	-136.1	-172.4	-174.5	-206.0	-235.7	-259.0	-286.6	-291.4	-287.9	-309.0	-337.0
Merchandise imports, adjusted	-108.3	-136.5	-136.8	-163.2	-187.9	-202.8	-221.6	-225.0	-227.0	-249.3	-273.2
Services payments	-13.3	-19.2	-19.8	-22.9	-25.4	-26.9	-27.5	-31.7	-31.7	-33.5	-36.6
Royalties and license fees payments	-0.1	-0.2	-0.2	-0.3	-0.4	-0.5	-0.5	-0.6	-0.7	-0.8	-0.9
Direct investment payments	-1.0	-1.8	-1.6	-0.6	-0.4	-1.1	-0.4	1.2	2.4	2.3	1.1
U.S. assets abroad, net	-14.5	-5.1	-3.0	-26.3	-14.2	-47.5	-29.9	17.7	-1.2	-3.4	1.7
U.S. private assets, net	-11.3	-2.0	0.1	-25.6	-21.8	-49.4	-20.0	16.5	-4.0	-2.1	0.0
U.S. direct investment abroad	-2.0	0.5	-0.7	-0.7	-2.3	-2.1	-0.6	-1.7	-0.5	-5.3	-8.3
Foreign securities	-0.8	1.7	0.7	10.7	9.5	1.0	3.8	-3.6	-7.2	-6.3	-13.5
Claims on unaffiliated foreigners	-0.2	-0.1	0.5	-0.4	0.4	0.1	-0.5	-0.8	-0.6	0.0	0.0
Claims reported by U.S. banks	-7.0	-1.1	-0.7	-34.7	-29.0	-49.3	-21.9	26.5	7.9	9.5	24.3
Foreign assets in the United States, net	6.8	21.0	35.6	65.5	52.5	98.8	46.2	-21.8	23.7	55.7	64.0
Foreign official assets in the United States, net	NA	NA	NA	NA	NA	NA	NA	NA	NA	NA	NA
Other foreign assets in the United States, net	NA	NA	NA	NA	NA	NA	NA	NA	NA	NA	NA
Foreign direct investment in the United States	1.9	5.6	3.8	7.5	9.9	19.2	20.2	18.6	11.7	4.0	1.8
U.S. Treasury securities	NA	NA	NA	NA	NA	NA	NA	NA	NA	NA	NA
Securities other than U.S. Treasury securities	1.3	1.5	6.4	15.5	13.9	9.4	13.1	-3.3	12.0	5.0	27.9
Liabilities to unaffiliated foreigners	-0.1	-0.9	0.9	-0.8	2.2	1.3	1.8	3.9	-0.2	1.5	NA
Liabilities reported by U.S. banks	3.8	14.6	24.2	42.4	28.7	68.8	10.3	-43.3	-1.1	43.1	31.1

*Data include Africa.

Source: *Survey of Current Business*, various issues.

TABLE 16. U.S. International Transactions: Asia*
($Billions)

	1983	1984	1985	1986	1987	1988	1989	1990	1991	1992	1993
Exports of goods, services, and income	75.3	76.3	70.5	71.8	81.6	102.9	111.6	123.4	135.8	147.0	156.4
Merchandise exports, adjusted	44.8	44.8	41.1	42.2	49.5	68.0	76.1	79.2	90.3	97.9	105.2
Services receipts	18.6	17.8	18.1	19.7	20.7	20.9	22.3	26.9	31.3	35.2	36.9
Royalties and license fees receipts	0.3	0.4	0.4	0.5	0.6	0.8	1.0	1.2	1.3	1.5	1.7
Income receipts on U.S. assets abroad	11.9	13.6	11.3	9.8	11.4	13.9	13.2	17.3	14.3	13.9	14.3
Direct investment receipts	5.3	6.0	4.4	3.3	5.3	5.8	6.3	8.0	8.4	9.3	9.8
Other private receipts	4.3	5.0	4.2	3.6	3.4	4.2	5.3	5.2	4.5	3.3	3.3
Imports of goods, services, and income	-83.5	-99.3	-94.4	-106.3	-128.4	-140.9	-159.1	-168.2	-167.0	-184.8	-200.9
Merchandise imports, adjusted	-65.0	-76.3	-71.2	-82.4	-103.3	-113.0	-128.1	-134.7	-134.7	-151.9	-166.0
Services payments	-8.8	-12.8	-13.2	-14.1	-15.8	-16.4	-16.7	-19.3	-18.5	-20.0	-21.6
Royalties and license fees payments	0.0	0.0	0.0	0.0	0.0	0.0	0.0	0.0	0.0	0.0	0.0
Direct investment payments	0.0	0.0	0.0	0.1	0.2	0.3	0.3	0.2	0.3	0.5	0.1
U.S. assets abroad, net	-11.2	-6.0	2.1	-0.8	2.9	-5.9	-4.9	-4.4	8.9	-18.3	-16.1
U.S. private assets, net	-7.9	-3.0	3.7	-0.3	0.8	-9.0	-6.6	-8.8	7.8	-18.0	-16.9
U.S. direct investment abroad	-1.0	0.2	-0.3	-0.3	-1.2	-1.0	-0.3	-0.8	-0.2	-4.4	-7.0
Foreign securities	-0.4	0.2	1.3	2.8	3.2	0.5	1.1	-1.5	4.0	-2.7	-11.2
Claims on unaffiliated foreigners	0.1	0.0	0.4	0.0	0.3	-0.4	-0.4	-0.2	-0.4	0.2	NA
Claims reported by U.S. banks	-5.3	-0.4	2.0	-2.2	-1.1	-8.9	-6.3	-2.3	8.0	-11.2	1.6
Foreign assets in the United States, net	-0.1	4.4	4.2	14.5	8.5	12.4	22.5	2.7	21.4	39.3	24.6
Foreign official assets in the United States, net	NA	NA	NA	NA	NA	NA	NA	NA	NA	NA	NA
Other foreign assets in the United States, net	NA	NA	NA	NA	NA	NA	NA	NA	NA	NA	NA
Foreign direct investment in the United States	0.2	1.2	0.4	0.5	1.1	2.0	1.5	-0.2	1.1	0.1	-0.4
U.S. Treasury securities	NA	NA	NA	NA	NA	NA	NA	NA	NA	NA	NA
Securities other than U.S. Treasury securities	0.4	0.2	0.7	2.7	1.2	0.1	3.5	-1.0	5.1	9.1	12.2
Liabilities to unaffiliated foreigners	-0.3	-1.1	0.4	-1.3	0.9	0.1	1.3	2.1	-0.6	0.8	NA
Liabilities reported by U.S. banks	-0.5	3.5	2.3	11.8	7.5	10.3	15.5	-0.4	15.0	27.7	10.8

*Data include Africa.

Source: *Survey of Current Business*, various issues.

TABLE 17. U.S. International Transactions: Japan
($Billions)

	1983	1984	1985	1986	1987	1988	1989	1990	1991	1992	1993
Exports of goods, services, and income	31.8	35.1	33.6	42.9	47.6	63.3	77.6	84.8	84.1	80.8	80.1
Merchandise exports, adjusted	21.8	23.2	22.1	26.4	27.6	37.2	43.9	47.8	47.2	46.9	46.9
Services receipts	6.1	7.4	7.6	11.1	12.9	15.4	19.0	21.9	24.8	26.1	27.1
Royalties and license fees receipts	0.9	1.0	1.1	1.4	1.9	2.5	2.7	3.0	3.4	3.5	4.0
Income receipts on U.S. assets abroad	3.9	4.4	3.8	5.5	7.0	10.7	14.8	15.1	12.1	7.9	6.1
Direct investment receipts	0.8	0.8	0.8	1.7	2.0	2.6	2.1	1.7	2.6	2.0	1.8
Other private receipts	2.9	3.4	2.9	3.4	4.9	8.1	12.3	12.4	8.2	5.0	3.7
Imports of goods, services, and income	-52.6	-73.1	-80.1	-99.7	-107.3	-118.1	-127.5	-123.2	-120.9	-124.2	-136.1
Merchandise imports, adjusted	-43.3	-60.2	-65.7	-80.8	-84.6	-89.8	-93.5	-90.4	-92.3	-97.4	-107.3
Services payments	-4.6	-6.4	-6.6	-8.7	-9.7	-10.5	-10.7	-12.3	-13.3	-13.5	-15.1
Royalties and license fees payments	-0.1	-0.2	-0.2	-0.3	-0.3	-0.4	-0.5	-0.6	-0.7	-0.8	-0.9
Direct investment payments	-1.0	-1.9	-1.5	-0.8	-0.6	-1.4	-0.7	1.0	2.1	1.8	1.0
U.S. assets abroad, net	-3.2	0.9	-5.1	-25.5	-17.0	-41.6	-25.0	22.1	-10.2	14.9	17.8
U.S. private assets, net	-3.4	1.0	-3.6	-25.3	-22.6	-40.4	-13.4	25.3	-11.8	15.9	16.9
U.S. direct investment abroad	-1.0	0.2	-0.3	-0.3	-1.2	-1.0	-0.3	-0.8	-0.2	-0.9	-1.3
Foreign securities	-0.4	1.5	-0.6	7.9	6.3	0.5	2.6	-2.1	-11.2	-3.6	-2.3
Claims on unaffiliated foreigners	-0.2	-0.1	0.1	-0.4	0.1	0.5	-0.1	-0.6	-0.3	-0.3	NA
Claims reported by U.S. banks	-1.8	-0.7	-2.7	-32.5	-27.9	-40.3	-15.6	28.9	-0.1	20.6	22.7
Foreign assets in the United States, net	6.9	16.6	31.4	51.0	44.0	86.4	23.6	-24.4	2.3	16.3	39.4
Foreign official assets in the United States, net	NA	NA	NA	NA	NA	NA	NA	NA	NA	NA	NA
Other foreign assets in the United States, net	NA	NA	NA	NA	NA	NA	NA	NA	NA	NA	NA
Foreign direct investment in the United States	1.6	4.4	3.4	7.0	8.8	17.2	18.7	18.8	10.7	4.0	2.2
U.S. Treasury securities	NA	NA	NA	NA	NA	NA	NA	NA	NA	NA	NA
Securities other than U.S. Treasury securities	0.9	1.3	5.7	12.8	12.7	9.3	9.6	-2.3	6.9	-4.1	15.8
Liabilities to unaffiliated foreigners	0.2	0.2	0.6	0.4	1.3	1.2	0.5	1.8	0.4	0.6	NA
Liabilities reported by U.S. banks	4.3	11.1	21.9	30.7	21.3	58.5	-5.2	-42.9	-16.1	15.4	20.3

Source: *Survey of Current Business*, various issues.

China's Rising Military Power and Influence

Robert Sutter

Summary

The power and influence of China's military, known as the People's Liberation Amy (PLA), is rising. U.S. policymakers are interested in this rise in several key areas:

1. *Leadership Politics and Policymaking*. The most coherent instrument of power in the People's Republic of China (PRC), the PLA is a possible arbiter should central civilian leaders reach an impasse over policy or leadership succession. PLA leaders may be more nationalistic and conservative than civilian counterparts in their support for China's security, sovereignty and stability, but they rigorously adhere to existing regime policies and show little extraordinary ambition for political leadership.

2. *Internal Stability*. The PLA is dedicated to guaranteeing China's internal security. It faces a society whose values are increasingly at odds with its own. Its ability to deal with this friction is complicated by modern influences and social problems (e.g., corruption, bribery, influence brokering) prevalent within the PLA.

3. *Economic Policy*. PLA leaders support and benefit from current economic policy. Many would like to garner more immediate benefit from China's rising economy, but generally PLA leaders seem to accept their assigned budget allocations.

4. *International Security Policy*:

- China's current military capabilities generally show little sign of China posing a serious threat to the United States for a decade or longer;

- The main danger spots over the next few years focus on contested territory in the Asian-Pacific region; examples include the South China Sea. Taiwan, and others;
- Perceived Chinese expansionist designs to control these contested areas are currently held in check by limitations in China's military capabilities; insufficient justification in terms of important Chinese interests; and likely negative foreign reaction. Each of these factors is subject to change.
- and PRC military leaders want to develop closer bilateral contacts for their own interests. At present, neither side sees the other as a strategic enemy, although each values "engagement" partly as a hedge against negative military action by the other.

INTRODUCTION

The rise of China's power and influence has captured the attention of international observers, including Members of Congress. Legislation under consideration in the 104th Congress and hearings on China have focused particular attention on the power and influence of China's military forces, known collectively as the People's Liberation Army.[1]

A review of U.S. Government and specialist assessments of China's armed forces shows several areas of concern involving the PLA.[2] In particular, U.S. policymakers in Congress and elsewhere are interested in:

- The role of the PLA in Chinese leadership politics and policymaking;
- The PLA's role as a force for internal stability in China;
- The PLA's role in the Chinese economy; and
- The role of the PLA in Chinese international security policy and behavior, especially in the East Asian region.

What follows is an assessment of the above four areas. The study examines relatively briefly the first three areas, as background to a more in-depth examination of the debate and conflicting evidence over the role of the PLA in China's international security policy and whether or not the PLA actually poses a threat to U.S. security interests in Asian and world affairs.

[1] See, among others, CRS Issue Brief 94002.

[2] See the testimony of 10 witnesses at Senate Foreign Relations Committee hearings of October 11 and 12, 1995. This study used particularly the testimony of Ronald Montaperto and Al Wilhelm. In addition, it benefitted from consultations and interviews with 20 U.S. government and non-government specialists and government and non-government experts from China conducted in August-November 1995. To encourage those interviewed to be as forthcoming as possible with their comments, it was agreed that the consultations would not be for attribution.

This report concludes with an overview of U.S. policy implications and options. An appendix provides a brief run-down on the current PLA forces.

THE ROLE OF THE PLA IN CHINESE LEADERSHIP POLITICS AND POLICYMAKING[3]

In Chinese domestic politics, the People's liberation Army (PLA) remains the ultimate instrument of central control over society and possibly resisting localities. At the same time, the PLA remains important as a possible arbiter should central, civilian policymakers reach an impasse on sensitive decision points involving domestic or foreign policies. PLA leaders may be more conservative than civilian counterparts in their support for nationalistic goals including states sovereignty, territorial integrity and internal security. But they adhere to existing regime policies and practices and evidence little sign of extraordinary ambition for political power.

The Army today is leaner, led by more professionally competent officers, and less inclined to identify with local interests than in the past. In the past 15 years, the PLA has gone through a series of important changes and reforms under senior leader Deng Xiaoping's direction. These have involved:

- Rotation of local military commanders.
- The establishment of more regular retirement of senior level leaders.
- Reduction in the number of military regions.
- Increased centralization of the chain-of-command.
- Big cuts in force levels (over one million men), along with incremental efforts to modernize the training, equipment and personnel procedures of the PLA.

At the last (14th) Party Congress in 1992, PLA leaders thought to have strong political ambitions were emoted in ways designed to firm up the principle of civil control of the military and reduce the chances of the emergence of a rival base of power. The consensus on the policies of economic reform and political authoritarianism reached at the Congress and later leadership meetings also suggested that the PLA leadership was prepared to adhere to and support current policies.

---

[3] Analysis in this section is taken in particular from discussion at the Institute for International Security Studies and China Association of Policy Studies conference on the PLA, June 1993; Swaine, Michael, "The Military and Political Succession in China," Rand Corp., 1992; discussion at the Third Japan-U.S. conference on China, July 1993, and discussion at the U.S. Defense Department Net Assessment Office, Conference on China's Future, August 1994. For background, see Kan, Shirley, *China's Military: Roles and Implications for U.S. Policy Toward China*, CRS Report 91-731F, October 3, 1991. See also the paper by David Shambaugh delivered at the PLA Towards 2000 Conference, Hong Kong, July 1995, forthcoming in *China Quarterly*.

Analysts, however, do not rule out an extraordinary intervention by the PLA in the political process. For one thing, it seems likely that the death of Deng Xiaoping will remove the leader with the most civilian and military prestige and create a power vacuum that will be difficult to fill. Few of the apparent contenders for power have extensive PLA experience. For the most part, party-government leaders and PLA leaders are following different career paths that make communications between the two more difficult. Thus, to achieve their interests, PLA leaders may feel compelled to resort to -- albeit reluctantly -- unauthorized actions. Secondly, politically ambitious PLA leaders who were demoted at the last Congress are still in the leadership or still retain considerable political influence; they may try to revive their political fortunes.

Against this backdrop, it is quite possible that a combination of factors such as policy indecision in Beijing and instability or disturbances in the provinces could provide sufficient justification for at least some PLA leaders to intervene in politics. Such intervention would be harder to stop in the absence of a senior leader like Deng Xiaoping. How intervention might take place is difficult to foresee. Some suggest that the size and difficulty of administering China would force the military to work through existing party-government authority. A serious danger posed by any such military intervention would arise if competing military leaders were vying for power. In such a case, a split in the PLA would presumably reflect a split in the leadership as a whole and add greatly to the administrative difficulties of ruling the country.

There have been a number of reports from party meetings in Beijing in late 1995 that Party Chairman Jiang Zemin was able to gain the appointment of senior military leaders associated with him to senior policy positions in the military. Examples include the appointment of Defense Minister Chi Haotien and General Zhang Wannian, the outgoing chief of general staff, to senior positions in the Party's policymaking Central Military Commission; and the appointment of General Fu Quanyou as the new chief of the general staff. These developments do not negate the underlying reality that there remains insufficient civilian control over the Chinese military, at least by standards prevalent in the West.[4]

The real chain-of-command over the military runs directly from the Politburo and the Chairman of Military Affairs Commission (MAC) of the Chinese Communist Party to the Secretary General of the MAC to the Chief-of-Staff and the operational commands of the military. The Ministry of National Defense exists in name only. Thus, China's military apparatus is an instrument of the Communist Party, not the government. A core mission of the People's Liberation Army (PLA) is to protect the Party and keep it in office. The PLA has unfettered, direct access to the top decisional body of the state.[5] This formal structure is reminiscent of the arrangement in Germany until World War I and Japan until World War II.

---

[4] For background, see CRS Issue Brief 93114.

[5] See notably paper given by Michel Oksenberg at Aspen Institute meeting on China, September 1995.

Of course, power at the apex of Chinese politics is rooted more in individuals than institutions and to assess the real influence and role of the military requires analysis of the informal linkages between the military and civilian sectors.[6] But from this vantage point, the conclusion is also clear: military-based networks are spreading into major sectors. Private corporations are being established with intimate links to the military. Their boards of directors and officers are drawn heavily from the military. In sum, whether viewed from the perspective of formal institutional arrangements or informal politics, the Chinese military will remain a major factor in domestic politics for decades to come.

Many within the military consider the PLA to be the defender of national values, China's sovereignty, and its unity.[7] Given its cohesion relative to other Chinese leadership institutions, its sense of mission regarding maintaining national unity and stability and defending China's interests abroad, and its strong position in the formal and informal mechanisms of Chinese policy and decisionmaking, the PLA's interests and policy preferences are important factors in Chinese behavior. Most notably, PLA leaders are thought to be in the forefront of Chinese leaders arguing for a firm posture against perceived encroachments or threats to Chinese sovereignty, involving such sensitive issues as Taiwan, Hong Kong, Tibet and the South China Sea. PLA leaders also are reported to be advocates of a firm PRC stance regarding unauthorized dissent and policies designed to ensure domestic stability. Finally, PLA leaders argue with some effect that China's military has been shortchanged in post-Mao distribution of resources and needs more material support in order to keep pace with the military modernization underway throughout the East Asian region.

THE PLA AND CHINA'S INTERNAL STABILITY[8]

A focal point of analytical concern in the West recently has been the nature of regime-society relations in China. If there is going to be a big challenge to China's new leaders and a major change in direction in Chinese policy and practice, many analysis believe it will be ignited by friction as the regime's injunctions and conflicting trends in the society rub together. Widespread discontent with growing official corruption has added fuel to this fire.

There has been mounting evidence of discontent in both rural and urban areas. Many city dwelling intellectuals, workers, and others were thought to have been seriously alienated from government authority following the repression of

[6] The PLA's representation in important political institutions is substantial. At present, military members of the Central Committee comprise 23 percent of the total membership of that body. Moreover, the PLA is also represented on the CCP Politburo, on the Standing Committee of the Politburo, and on key Leading Small Groups concerned with foreign affairs and broad national security policy.

[7] See paper by Michel Oksenberg, prepared for the Aspen Strategy Group, August 1995.

[8] For background, see CRS Report 95-465S, pp. 13-15.

the Tiananmen demonstrations of 1989. This has moderated over the years but not disappeared.

Urban dwellers also contain the largest groups in the society whose benefits are being fundamentally challenged by the economic reform policies. They are not used to economic insecurity and some are thought to be willing to restrict reform in order to preserve their benefits (e.g., guaranteed jobs, low-cost housing, health-care). Others likely welcome the enormous increase in personal freedom that comes from the breakdown of the so-called work unit system that has dominated the life of workers and others associated with state-controlled enterprises and other places of employment. In particular, the individual worker is no longer dependent on the unit and its sometimes capricious and overbearing leaders for the essentials of life (salary, housing, schooling for children, rations if applicable). On balance, it seems fair to conclude that most urban workers in state controlled enterprises--while they might welcome new freedom--are unused to and fearful of the possible negative consequences for them that could result from "jumping into the sea" of market-oriented enterprise in Chinese cities.

In the countryside, the terms of trade and government procurement practices for agricultural goods have taken a turn relatively disadvantageous for farmers after the high growth in peasant income fostered by government policies in the late 1970s and early 1980s. Prices of consumer goods and agricultural inputs have risen, far outpacing government procurement prices for agricultural commodities. Local officials responsible for purchasing grain and other mandated crops have sometimes used their allocations of cash to speculate in real estate or local enterprises. They have provided peasants with "IOUs" for their crops--a practice that has set off a number of peasant demonstrations and riots. Local officials have often established a sometimes dizzying array of taxes, fees and levies on the peasants in order to help support local services and to provide capital for entrepreneurial endeavors supported by local officials. The cumulative effect of all these practices has been large scale popular discontent and many reports of strikes, demonstrations and sometimes violent riots against local officials and the broader administrative system that supports them.

In the past, the center could endeavor to deal with such problems through party channels, using the so-called "rectification" campaigns to week out corrupt or abusive local officials in order to insure continued effective government. Current conditions in China make such an approach less likely to succeed. Reformers in Beijing are following policies that tacitly endorse the widespread "entrepreneurship" shown by local officials. The scope of corruption and misuse of funds has reportedly become so wide that there may not be enough untainted cadre or local officials uninvolved in these practices to replace or sanction the errant local cadre.

Behind this state of affairs rests a widespread cynical view of power and politics in China. In the past, the vision of Marxism-Leninism had created an important incentive to motivate part-government cadre to insure their loyalty to central discipline. Today that ideology is widely viewed as bankrupt, and has often been replaced by a more particularistic, self-serving mentality where cadre work hard to benefit mainly themselves, their families and their localities.

Democratic societies have established usually effective institutions to deal with local-central conflicts of interest and friction between the society and the state. China has few of these mechanisms. The policy consensus in Beijing seems to preclude any significant political reforms or changes to establish them in the near future. The result is likely to be continued friction between the society on the one hand and the organs and officials of government, especially central government, on the other.

ROLE OF THE PLA[9]

This state of affairs places heavy responsibility on the PLA, the ultimate instrument of central control over society. By any measure, the PLA is the most coherent of all of China's institutions. although its leaders may hold somewhat different views on a range of strategic, political, and economic issues, and although they may differ as they debate specific issues of force modernization, doctrine, or military operations, they are highly professional and increasingly capable military officers who exhibit a strong sense of corporate identity, and who share a strong sense of corporate interest. Owing to their strong nationalism and growing professional spirit, they are dedicated to the twin missions of defending China against external attach and guaranteeing the internal security of the nation. If China were to be threatened, either from without or within, the PLA would defend the unity of the Chinese state.

The PLA is arguably the most conservative of all of the major political groupings in contemporary Chinese society. China's military leaders are also aware of a growing disjunction between the values they espouse and those embraced by the mainstream of Chinese society.

The majority of PLA officers accept and support the prevailing PRC leadership goal of "Socialism with Chinese characteristics," a formulation that is so vague as to justify building an economy in which more than 80% of commodity prices are set by market mechanisms. They accept this approach partly because it produces the financial resources to support the military modernization program. At the same time, however, PLA leaders remain concerned by what they define as the negative consequences the implementation of this approach is having on socialist and especially traditional Chinese values and behavior.

Their apprehension is reinforced by an awareness that the untoward effects of current economic policies might, if left unanswered, result in a net increase in

---

9 See testimony of R. Montaperto, October 11, 1995, op. cit.

popular discontent and eventually threaten the stability of the larger social system. Corruption is high on the list of their concerns.

The major concern is that if popular discontent were to spread, become focused, and result in a new round of political demonstrations, the PLA would once again be called into the breach to restore order. Although they would almost certainly intervene if they were to judge the situation to be extreme, PLA officers likely wish to avoid a repeat of the 1989 Tiananmen repression which seriously reduced military prestige. The PLA action at Tiananmen also diverted attention away from what was then and is still considered to be the main professional task of the military today, building the capabilities that will better enable China to face the future.

Another problem facing the PLA is an inevitable consequence of professionalization, the emergence of an increasingly distinct line of demarcation between the military and the larger society. Under present circumstances, the separation is rendered even more distinct owing to the significant gap that exists between the economic, lifestyle, and prestige opportunities available to the civilian population and those available to military personnel. Officers at all levels, but particularly those in the lower grades, are frustrated by such income differentials and by their perception that the values to which they subscribe are not generally shared by members of the civilian sector. Meanwhile, social problems in other parts of Chinese society are also becoming common among the PLA. In particular, corruption pervades every aspect of Chinese politics. PLA officers and men frequently demonstrate that they are by no means unaware of the temptations of bribery and influence brokering. PLA leaders offer no realistic solution to the dilemma other than to try to build the proper spirit within the military ranks. Judging by the steady stream of exhortation, the result thus far has been mixed.

THE PLA AND CHINA'S ECONOMY[10]

PLA leaders actively support present economic policies which emphasize reducing the scope of the planned economy, a reliance on market mechanisms to set prices and structure distribution, and the devolution of economic power to lower administrative levels. Military support is based upon a reasoned judgment that such policies provide the best opportunity for the PLA eventually to acquire the capabilities to prosecute modern, high-technology warfare. Present economic policies are seen as the best means of achieving one of the most important of all of the PLA's corporate interests -- professionalization and modernization.

The PLA leadership accepts the principle, announced more than a decade ago, that military modernization and especially the acquisition of modern weap-

[10]Data and information in this section are taken from testimony of Al Wilhelm, October 11, 1995, op. cit; and to a lesser degree from testimony of R. Montaperto, October 11, 1995, op. cit.

onry must await the construction of a strong modern economy. Caught as they are between the perceived need for more, and their recognition of economic reality, they are forced to support the drive for continuing economic development. Like their civilian leaders who see economic development as the key to regime stability and longevity, the leaders of the PLA are betting on the proposition that building a strong economy is the best path towards developing modern military capabilities.

Within the PLA, balanced development is about as difficult to achieve as within the society at large, and similar levels of contention are generated as competing commands, mission elements, and strategies vie for finite resources. The allied victory in the Gulf War had a profound impact upon the thinking of China's military leaders. More than any other event, the rapid, successful conclusion of that conflict settled lingering questions about the proper direction for developing China's future military capabilities. The PLA is committed to building the mix of capabilities that will guarantee the successful prosecution of so-called Local Wars of Limited Duration. Preparation for such limited war is the first priority and will continue to be so for the foreseeable future, but strategic weapons and special operations cannot be neglected. Each of these areas requires significant new investment annually in the development of strategy, doctrine, and tactics; education and training; new or enhanced command, control communications and intelligence systems; research, development and procurement of at least a limited quantity of new weapons systems for testing, training and evaluation, and the logistics to support each. In the past decade the official defense budget has grown 314.2%, compared with an increase of 266% that would have been necessary to keep pace with inflation.

OFFICIAL DEFENSE BUDGET OF THE PRC

Year	Budget (bil RMB)	% Increase	Inflation Rate	% State Budget	% of GNP
1986	20.08	4.9	6.0	8.79	2.07
1987	20.96	4.4	6.0	8.64	1.85
1988	21.80	4.0	18.8	8.17	1.55
1989	25.15	15.4	17.8	8.56	1.57
1990	29.03	15.4	2.1	8.98	1.64
1991	33.03	13.8	2.9	8.70	1.63
1992	37.79	14.4	5.4	8.53	1.55
1993	43.25	14.4	13.2	7.64	1.38
1994	55.06	27.3	23.0	9.46	1.26
1995	63.10	14.6	15.0 (est)	9.92	1.32 (est)

Notes: Budget increase 1986-1995 - 314.2%; to keep pace with inflation the increase would be 266%; estimates are official PRC government estimates.[11]

PLA leaders say that approximately one-third of the official defense budget covers personnel cost, including basic salaries at approximately 3000 RMB ($345

[11] From testimony of Al Wilhelm, op. cit.

US) per solider, uniforms, and food staples. Another one-third is for Operations and Maintenance (O&M) costs, including very limited allocations for large unit exercises, steaming and flying time, and live-fire training. The last one-third is invested in military research and development (R&D), procurement, and major facilities. At the market exchange rate of 8.7 RMB/U.S. Dollar, the 1995 defense allocation equals about $7.25 billion. In spite of low salaries and the fact that the purchasing power of the RMB may be greater than the exchange rate would indicate, $7.25 billion dollars is not enough to field an army of three million troops. Most outside observers accept that the published budget of figures must be at least doubled.[12]

Arms sales by defense-related corporations are commonly viewed outside China as a major source of income. However, most major weapons makers are not owned or operated by the PLA, but by one of the civilian ministries. The proceeds from most foreign arms sales go to the originating ministry and not the PLA. Notable exceptions occur when the PLA sells from inventory or from a manufacturer owned by the PLA. Furthermore, a review of arms sales from 1985-1992 shows that China's arms sales averaged little more than $1.5 billion a year.[13] Even if the entire amount were profit that went to the PLA, the addition to the military's coffers would not be great. According to the PRC government, at least one-third of state-owned enterprises are operating at a loss and only one-third are breaking even. Arms industries are all state-owned and like the rest, many are unprofitable, and all are attempting to convert their excess capacity to civilian production. Of those making a profit, at least half of the profits are being reinvested in defense conversion or modernization as part of the state's massive effort to create new jobs. Finally, China's arms sales bottomed when the 1991 Gulf War's demonstration of high-tech weaponry's effectiveness undermined China's sales of lower-tech materials. With the dramatic drop in arm sales, central government revenue from such sales, at most is no longer -- if it ever were -- a major source of funding. This condition will likely continue well into the 21st Century. However, in the future Chinese sales could again be a growing factor in the international market as the quality of its weapons systems begin to catch up with international standards under the ongoing reforms.

The role of the PLA in jobs creation has been important to china's economic reforms. It will continue to be so until China has in place a social security system that empowers labor with mobility, and Beijing has effectively implemented a tax structure that supports the central government's revenue needs. By 2010, the PLA plans to have divested itself of the majority of its enterprises. The benefit will be an even more trim and professional force, having been reduced to approximately two million.

---

[12] See papers by Richard Betzinger and Chong-pin Lin given at the 4th Staunton Hill conference on the PLA, June 1995.

[13] Testimony of Al Wilhelm, op. cit.

The last major source of defense funding is the expenditures covered by local governments and the industrial ministries which, for example, absorb at least one half the costs of China's research and development (R&D). The central defense budget only pays the basic procurement or production costs for nuclear weapons and major conventional weapon systems (both domestic and foreign). The other costs are substantial, and as yet appear to be serviced sufficiently to ensure development of research and development. But as state enterprises are privatized, the pressure on the defense budget to fund these costs will increase accordingly.

In a word, the increases in resources made available to the PLA can easily be exaggerated. Likewise, what the PLA is able to do with these moneys is also subject to overestimation by some observers. The increases in funding in part have been used to finance the purchase of modern military equipment and military technologies from abroad, particularly from Russia. However, the quantities involved appear to be relatively small. Also, Chinese military modernization strategies do not place major emphasis on acquiring large quantities of equipment and material from foreign sources. Rather, the approach is to make smaller purchases, practice reverse engineering, and then use the knowledge gained to build indigenous capabilities.

It is most likely that the lion's share of the increases of the last few years has been used to compensate for very low defense budgets during the 1980s, to offset the effects of inflation for the last several years, and to improve the quality of life for the forces. For example, in 1994 there was an across-the-board increase in the monthly wages of all PLA officers, with those at the top receiving an increase of more than 40%. Thus, although the increases of the last six years have helped to lay a foundation for the future, they probably have not yet produced the desired increase in overall military capabilities. Such success as has been achieved has whetted the PLA appetite for more. China's military leaders are expected to continue to use all of their considerable political resources to increase the military budget. It is uncertain if they will be able to increase the share of military spending relative to the overall state budget and the overall level of GNP much beyond the levels prevalent in recent years.

THE PLA AND CHINA'S INTERNATIONAL SECURITY POLICY AND BEHAVIOR[14]

Chinese international security policy changed markedly during the Maoist period (1949-1976). It moved from reliance on the USSR and strident opposition to the United States to a posture of strong opposition to both the U.S. and the USSR and finally to an approach that relied strategically on reconciliation with the United States to deal with the danger posed by the Soviet threat. After Mao

[14] For background, see CRS Reports 95-465S, and 95-46S.

died, Chinese leaders emphasized domestic policies of development that required markedly increased economic contacts abroad and gave added impetus to Beijing's desire to sustain good relations with the West and avoid disruptions around the periphery of China that would complicate the Chinese drive toward modernization.

Major changes have taken place in the international balance of power since the late 1980s (e.g, the collapse of the Soviet Union) and in China (e.g., the Tiananmen crackdown), but Chinese foreign policy continues to adhere to the general outlines established in the years after Mao's death. So long as China remains preoccupied with internal developments and international actors avoid initiatives seen as posing fundamental challenges to the Chinese leadership, PRC leaders, including those of the PLA, seem likely to continue to follow the relatively narrow range of policies that they have adhered to in the past 15 years.

Several trends have characterized the Chinese approach to international security policy in the post-Mao period:

- Chinese leaders now face a security environment around China's periphery that is less likely to be disrupted by a major international power than at any time in the recent past.
- Regional security trends have been generally compatible with China's primary concern with internal economic modernization and political stability.
- Ideological and leadership disputes have had less importance for Chinese policy than in the past.
- Chinese policy has become more economically dependent on other countries, especially the Western-aligned, developed countries, than in the past. They have provided the assistance, technology, investment and markets China needs to modernize effectively.
- China's overall pragmatic adjustments to world affairs have not been dependent on just one or two leaders in China. Although Deng Xiaoping picked up senior foreign policymaking duties from Mao Zedong and Zhou Enlai, the policies followed represented, in broad terms, a consensus among senior Chinese leaders who have been advised and influenced by a wide range of experts and interest groups in China.

There remains the distinct possibility that outside forces (e.g., the U.S., Taiwan) may adopt policies that challenge fundamental Chinese interests and prompt a strongly assertive Chinese response. For example, Beijing has threatened repeatedly that it would resort to force if Taiwan declared independence of in the event of foreign interference in the island's affairs. Beijing also has shown willingness in recent years to assert Chinese nationalistic claims to territories also claimed by its neighbors, notably in the South China Sea. Some analysts judge in addition that Beijing may revert to a tough anti-U.S. posture if the United States escalates sanctions and other pressures on China's communist regime. Hostilities in Korea that threatened vital Chinese security interests also might prompt a forceful Chinese response.

PLA leaders have generally supported the broad outlines of China's international security policies in the post-Mao period. From time to time, reports surface in Hong Kong media and the Western press regarding the PLA's alleged push for a "harder" line on such sensitive issues as policy toward the South China Sea, Taiwan, and the United States. Interviews[15] with U.S. intelligence analysts who review these reports along with other information available to U.S. Government officials sometimes support the notion that the PLA leaders are more conservative and "hard line" on issues affecting national sovereignty and territorial integrity. But in general these U.S. analysts tend to see PLA leaders reflecting the consensus of views on sensitive international security policy issues at any given time. Thus, there are perceived to be about as many "hardliners" and "moderates" among PLA senior leaders on particular international issues as there are in the party-government structure as a whole. Of course, the relative weight of PLA opinion in international security policy issues will be affected by the importance of military force in dealing with a problem. Decisions on issues involving the possible use of force are seen to give the PLA more influence than those where the use of force is less likely.

Does the PLA Pose an Emerging Threat to U.S. Security Interests?[16]

Given the recent, generally moderate trend of Chinese international security policy away from the radical swings and frequent military confrontation in the three earlier decades of the PRC, the question arises as to why the PLA and its influence on China's policies and practices are seen by many outside observers as an emerging threat to U.S. security concerns.

Interviews with U.S. and international security affairs specialists and a review of the wide range of analyses and commentaries on China's military and related activities show that China's security threat to U.S. interests is seen in distinct and sometimes contradictory ways.[17]

a. *China's Military Threat*. There appears to be a general agreement among specialists that China, at present, does not pose a significant direct military

[15] Interviews, Washington, DC, October, November, 1995.

[16] See the detailed analysis and sources cited in CRS Report 95-46S.

[17] For background, see among others, *Jane's Intelligence Review*, April 1993, Vol. 5, No. 4., James Lilley. Testimony before House Foreign Affairs Committee, May 20, 1993. U.S.-Japan Policy Dialogue on China: Security Issues, Asia Society, 1993, 45 p. See also the work of Michael Swaine cited in footnote 3 and the article on China's military power by Thomas McNaugher published in *The Brookings Review*, summer 1994.

threat to the United States. Its military, economic and other capabilities are seen as too limited to pose such a danger in the near future (4-10 years). A number of knowledgeable U.S. and foreign analysts see potential for China to challenge and threaten the United States over the longer term (20-plus years). Of the nations of the world, in their view, China is among the very few that have the mix of economic, political, and military factors that could lead to the emergence of national power capable of directly challenging the United States in the first half of the 21st Century.

In the interim, the main danger for U.S. interests coming from China focuses on U.S. interests in preserving and strengthening the peace and stability of the Asian-Pacific region. There is considerable debate among specialists as to whether or not China is likely to embark on an expansionist course disruptive to stability in the area (see discussion below).

b. *China as a proliferator of weapons of mass destruction, manufacturing technology for such weapons, and related delivery systems.* Chinese military strategy against both the United States and the Soviet Union focused during much of the Maoist period (1949-1976) on developing reliable, hard-to-locate weapon systems of mass destruction -- i.e., nuclear missiles and bombs. These weapons gave Chinese leaders the option of a second strike against a stronger adversary and thus were seen to deter a feared preemptive nuclear attack, especially from the USSR. For many years, China shared such technology with a select group of countries, notably Pakistan, whose defense had a direct bearing on China's own national security. At the same time, China has a long record of selling materials, technology, and related expertise in these sensitive areas for profit. The PLA was in charge of implementing these policies and practices.

In the past, U.S. and other western-aligned international observers tended to play down the consequences of these Chinese actions. They appeared more interested in sustaining a broadly cooperative relationship with Beijing in the Cold War competition with the Soviet Union. U.S. views changed markedly in the post-Cold War environment. This occurred especially after the 1991-1992 U.S.-led allied confrontation with Iraq, which was suspected of developing mass destruction weapons in order to dominate world oil supplies. Fearful of having to confront authoritarian, expansionist leaders armed with nuclear or other mass destruction weapons and related delivery systems, U.S. officials now saw China's proliferation practices as a major threat to U.S. interests.[18] American officials have had some success in recent years in leading international efforts to press China to adhere to international control regimes regarding nuclear weapons and related missile delivery systems. In this effort, they have used leverage provided by China's dependence on trade and other relations with the U.S. and other developed countries concerned with proliferation.

---

[18]See notably CRS Report 95-46S.

The PLA has gone along with the PRC leadership consensus on proliferation. Where Chinese proliferation against established international norms takes place, it is generally viewed by experts as a result of the policies of the Chinese leadership as a whole. The view of the PLA as a "rogue" element, engaging in nuclear, missile and other proliferation out of the oversight and not subjected to the influence of China's leaders, enjoys only a limited following among China specialists.[19]

c. *China's Economic Threat* The strength, size, and vibrancy of the Chinese economy has attracted positive international attention but also has caused considerable uneasiness among China's major trading partners. Although China's economy also was large and grew rapidly in the Maoist period, the regime's "self-reliant" development strategy meant that Chinese interaction with the world economy was limited, and therefore the consequences of developments in China for other nations were generally not large.

The post-Mao economic reforms have changed that situation. On the one hand, the Chinese economy is larger than ever and is growing at a rate surpassing that of the Maoist period and mirroring the rapid rise that some other Asian countries experienced during periods of economic "take off" in the latter 20th century. At the same time, the Chinese "open door" policies have put aside Maoist autarchy in favor of integrating the Chinese economy with the growing economies of Asia and the world. In the past 15 years, Chinese foreign trade and foreign investment in China have grown at rates far surpassing China's overall economic growth rate. The Chinese economy today depends more on foreign trade than do the economies of other large countries like Russia, India and Brazil, and that dependency even surpasses that of the United States and Japan. China is now among the top 15 world traders and rising fast. Much of the trade stems from investment from inside China and from abroad in manufacturing industries designed to produce goods for export. To a considerable degree, China has become a manufacturing platform for exports to many countries of the world.

Against this background, analysts in Asia and the West sometimes see China's economic power and potential as a current or prospective threat to Asian stability or the stability of international commerce in certain commodities. On the one hand, Chinese leaders may choose to use this rapid economic growth to support military modernization and a more assertive policy toward China's neighbors. On the other hand, Chinese enterprises may choose to direct their manufacturing capabilities to world markets sensitive to the rest of Asia and the West.

In this view, the size, scope, and capabilities of the Chinese economy, when combined with the fact that the economic system in China remains subject to state control and direction in several important respects, means that China is

[19] Interviews, Washington, D.C., August-November 1995.

seen as having a great ability to "surge." This involves targeting production in certain areas, dominating markets, and causing major disruption and dislocation for trading partners and competitors. Of course, the larger and more resilient world economies (e.g., the United States, Japan) doubtless are better able to adjust to Chinese growth, but others (e.g., Taiwan) may find themselves too small and vulnerable to adjust gracefully to a directed or predatory Chinese economic initiative.

As noted above, the PLA plays a role in the Chinese economy and Chinese economic decisionmaking. Why and how the PLA would push Chinese international economic policy and behavior in more threatening or confrontational directions remains largely unexplored. This is presumably because there are few data available on PLA thinking on this issue, and because the PLA's influence on Chinese economic policy has been seen as more limited than in other policy areas (e.g., national security).

d. *The Threat of a Weakened China.* Seemingly at odds with above lines of analyses, which stress China's growing military or economic power, is the view held by some prominent specialists in Asia and the West who worry about the dangers to Asian stability posed by a markedly weakened China. the concern focuses on a possible breakdown in government authority in China, such as was seen in a number of Communist countries in recent years. The size and scope of problems in China suggest that such a breakdown could be accompanied by large scale economic dislocation, armed conflict, and massive outflows of migrants. For the crowded and often strongly homogeneous countries along China's eastern rim, and for the sparsely populated and poorly controlled countries to China's north and west, such outflows of migrants would pose a national security threat of the first order. Asian analysts recall the massive difficulties caused to the relatively less crowded countries of Southeast Asia by the exodus of one million "boat people" from Vietnam in the late 1970s and early 1980s. They expect that since China's population today is 20 times that of Vietnam at that time, any significant outflow from China would have major consequences for the entire region. As noted above, the PLA's interests and policy role would likely see the military intervene to prevent such collapse, support existing authority, and preserve social stability.

Factors Favoring Viewing China as a Current or Emerging Threat

Several developments in recent years have contributed to a view of China as an emerging threat to U.S. security interests. They involve China's accelerated military buildup and expanding armed presence, assertive warnings and military maneuvers concerning some disputes, and history of using force to settle disputes. They can be divided into two broad groups: developments in China's military capabilities, and developments in Chinese intentions.

Capabilities

Higher Priority for Defense/Growth in Defense Spending

As noted in the section on the PLA and China's economy, China's defense spending has grown markedly since the PLA played a key role in cracking down on political dissent at Tiananmen Square and other parts of China in 1989. Analysts have viewed the spending increase partly as a reflection of party leaders' concern to beef up the capabilities and insure the loyalty of the PLA during a period of crisis. By 1990, the Communist leadership was no longer speaking of military modernization as something that would follow economic modernization, as had been the case for most of the previous decade. Rather, the party leadership endorsed increased efforts in national defense along with economic development.[20]

The end of the Cold War and collapse of the Soviet Union by 1991 were duly noted by Chinese planners but resulted in no slackening in Chinese defense increases. Reports suggested that Chinese planners were alarmed by the results of the 1991-1992 Persian Gulf War, which showed how backward and vulnerable Iraqi forces were in the face of modern western firepower. there were many parallels between Iraqi and Chinese force structures, and Beijing planners were reportedly determined to use increased spending to modernize the abilities of their forces to deal with Western arms.

Acquisitions of Foreign Advanced Weapons

China has been able to channel some of its increased defense budget and substantial hard currency earnings to procurement of advanced weapons abroad. Denied U.S. arms since 1989, China has purchased Russian fighters, other aircraft, and other more advanced weapons technology. Russian arms sales in 1991-92 to China totaled about $2 billion. In fall 1993, a five-year military cooperation agreement was signed which was expected to significantly broaden the transfer of military technology to China. The Chinese reportedly were permitted to recruit large numbers (over 1,000) of Russian weapons scientists to work in China, notably in research institutes under the Aeronautics Ministry. Meanwhile, hundreds of Chinese defense scientists reportedly have been working at Russian aerospace institutes.[21] Significant Israeli transfers to China have also been reported.[22]

---

[20] For background about development of the Chinese military up to late 1991, see *China's Military: Roles and Implications for U.S. Policy Toward China*, by Shirley Kan, CRS Report 91-731F, October 3, 1991.

[21] John Fialka, "U.S. Faces China's Success in Skimming Cream of Weapons Experts From Russia," the *Wall Street Journal*, October 14, 1993, p. A12; the *New York Times*, November 10, 1993; *Jane's Defense Weekly*, February 19, 1994.

[22] The CIA's response to questions from the Senate Governmental Affairs Committee (hearing date February 24, 1993) states that more than a decade of acquiring defense technologies from Israel may have cost China "several

China is believed to be focused on obtaining a greater power-projection capability, centered on superior air cover and a blue-water Navy. In addition, sales to China of advanced missile and nuclear technology (from Russia) pose concerns for U.S. policymakers, in part because of the potential for retransfer to buyers of Chinese supplies.

Some consider China's arms purchases to be the cause of an imbalance of power in Asia, particularly in the Taiwan Strait.[23] Arms sales, such as U.S. F-16A/B and French Mirage fighters, to Taiwan are meant to deter Chinese aggression and maintain stability, they say.

Reports of major PLA acquisitions since 1990 have been included:[24]

- Mil Mi17 helicopters from the Soviet Union
- Su-27 Soviet fighters from Russia worth about $1 billion, based at Wuhu (100 km south of Nanjing); negotiating an additional 26 Su-27s, including acquiring domestic production rights--some reports confirm the sale.
- Kilo-class conventional submarines from Russia
- I1-76 heavy transport planes from Russia--some reports note plans to purchase more.
- T-72 tanks from Russia
- Patriot missile technology (allegedly from Israel)
- In-flight refueling technology (perhaps from Israel, Russia, or Iran)
- Up to 100 Russian S-300 surface-to-air missiles (similar to the Patriot), with 4 mobile launchers
- Rocket engines and missile guidance technology from Russia
- Uranium enrichment technology and nuclear reactors from Russia
- AEW (airborne early warning), missile (SSMs, SAMs, and AAMs), and tank armor technology from Israel and/or Russia.
- Stinger anti-aircraft missiles (perhaps from Pakistan)
- Klimov/Sarkisov RD33 jet engines from Russia
- Avionics for F-8II fighters from the U.S. (delivery in December 1992 for pre-1989 sale)

billion dollars." The Israeli Prime Minister on October 13, 1993, acknowledged Israeli arms sales to China, estimating their value in 1992 to be $60 million.

[23] Michael T. Klare, "The Next Great Arms Race," *Foreign Affairs* (summer 1993), highlights a competition for advanced arms in Asia and that "the China-Taiwan nexus probably constitutes the most vibrant arms market in the world today."

[24] In addition to coverage in prominent western daily media, useful sources for the following information included the *Far Eastern Economic Review*, various *Jane's* publications, the *Asian Wall Street Journal*, and *The Economist*.

- Artillery munitions production equipment from the U.S. (delivery in December 1992 for pre-1989 sale)
- AN/TPQ-37 artillery locating radars from the U.S. (final delivery in December 1992 for pre-1989 sale)
- Mark 45 MOD 2 anti-submarine torpedoes from the U.S. (delivery in December 1992 for pre-1989 sale).

In addition, China reportedly has been discussing other weapons purchases:

- MiG-31 fighters from Russia (may include production technology)
- Tu-22M bomber (4,000km range, air-refueling capability) from Russia
- I1-76 airborne warning and control system aircraft from Russia
- AEW (airborne early-warning) system possibly from Russia
- Aircraft carrier possibly from Russia, France.

Expanded Military Presence In Asia. Recent military construction by the PLA has indicted a continued strategy to expand military influence over the contested waters in Southeast Asia. A notable example was recently discovered shelters in Mischief Reef, an area claimed notably by the Philippines. China's efforts to expand its military presence in contested areas increase the chances of armed conflict with Asian neighbors. Meanwhile, Beijing has initiated a series of large military exercises in the general area of Taiwan, presumably with the intent to curb movement toward separatism by political leaders on Taiwan.[25]

The PLA has reportedly deployed three Romeo-class submarines from the North Sea Fleet to the South Sea Fleet, in order to patrol the disputed south China Sea.[26] In June 1992, China signed an oil exploration agreement with the American company, Crestone Energy Corp., for an area in the south China Sea claimed also by Vietnam. Such a venture might provide the PLA with a pretext to act militarily in the disputed waters. Crestone's chairman stated that Chinese officials assured the company that it will be protected with China's "full naval might."[27] Thus far, there has been no subsequent military conflict over these actions. china also has built an airbase on one of the Paracel Islands (Woody Island) in order to extend its air patrol capability over the Spratlys.[28] It has built military installations on reefs claimed by the Philippines, among others. China's new kilo subs have been reported in the Taiwan Strait, while its SU-27s have been reported at the South China Sea area, Hainan Island.[29]

---

[25] *Far Eastern Economic Review*, October 13, 1994, CRS Report 95-968S.

[26] *Far Eastern Economic Review*, April 8, 1993, p. 9.

[27] Nicholas D. Kristof, "China Signs U.S. Oil Deal for Disputed Waters," the *New York Times*, June 18, 1992, p. A8.

[28] *Far Eastern Economic Review* August 13, 1992, p. 16.

[29] Interview, December 1995.

There are also signs that China is seeking to obtain a military presence close to the Indian Ocean, through its close friend and arms recipient, Burma. China was reported building a base for Burma on an island in the Bassein River, Close to India's Andaman Islands. According to Japanese sources, the PLA would be able to use the facility. In addition, China was reported to be constructing a radar station on the Coco Islands, north of the Andamans.[30] The current status of these reported endeavors is unclear.

Ballistic Missiles and Nuclear Weapons. China is continuing to modernize its nuclear forces, called the Second Artillery. China's nuclear testing shows a determined program to upgrade its nuclear weapons and improve their survivability, accuracy and safety. China's nuclear tests have continued in spite of a global moratorium on nuclear testing by the United States, Russia, and the United Kingdom in an effort to achieve a comprehensive nuclear test ban. President Clinton has repeatedly expressed disappointment at Chinese testing. The United States welcomed China's recent declaration that it will abide by a comprehensive nuclear test ban agreement proposed for 1996.[31]

China is believed to be developing new ballistic missile systems with improved accuracy and guidance, greater range, and multiple warheads. A new supersonic bomber, Hong-7, is under development. A more advanced submarine launched ballistic missile, Julang-2, is also being developed.[32] Some believe that China is developing new tactical as well as strategic nuclear warheads. The Chinese have developed the M-9 (600 km) and M-11 (300 km) short-range ballistic missiles that can have nuclear or conventional warheads. Chinese doctrine on the use of tactical nuclear weapons has not been clear.[33]

INTENTIONS

Regional Dominance/Global Influence

Many believe that China's goals in building up its military include gaining regional dominance, in the sense that China would have influence or control over developments in Asia. China's views on regional developments, however, may conflict with the interests of the United States and its allies, such as Japan. Adhering to a balance of power perspective on world politics, many Chinese leaders see building China's military capability as necessary in the face of Russian, Japanese, and U.S. influence in Asia. In addition, the lessons of the Persian Gulf War, as perceived by them, are that modern warfare requires high-tech weapons. According to this view, China can be expected to use military power

[30] *The Economist*, October 22, 1992, p. 1.

[31] The *New York Times*, September 18, 1993. See also CRS Report 94-422S, *Chinese Nuclear Weapons and Arms Control Policies*, March 25, 1994.

[32] See, for example, *Bulletin of the Atomic Scientists*, November 1993.

[33] Richard Fieldhouse, "China's Mixed Signals on Nuclear Weapons," *Bulletin of the Atomic Scientists*, May 1991.

(including upgraded nuclear capability) to back its political claims to world power status and to support Chinese foreign policy efforts to check U.S. global influence when it conflicts with Chinese aspirations.[34]

Actions on Sovereignty Disputes and Offshore Resources

China has issued warnings on the possible use of force to settle several disputes, including the South China Sea, Taiwan, and Hong Kong. Chinese claims to much of the South China Sea extend close to Southeast Asian countries and include the contested Spratly and Paracel Islands.[35] Taiwan, Vietnam, the Philippines, Malaysia, and Brunei also claim all or part of the Spratlys, while Vietnam and Taiwan also claim the Paracels.[36] In addition to disputes in the South China Sea, Japan (a U.S. ally), Taiwan, and China have claimed the Diaoyu (in Chinese) or Senkaku (in Japanese) Islands. Tensions increased in February 1992, when China issued a Territorial Waters Law formally declaring Chinese sovereignty over disputed areas, including the South China Sea and Diaoyu/Senkaku Islands. The law also specifically authorized the PLA to enforce the claims by force. Subsequent Chinese statements seeking to settle the disputes peacefully and to abide by the Law of the Sea and other norms have eased regional concerns to some degree, although Chinese military actions in the South China Sea and Taiwan Strait are a continuing source of concern.

While the PRC has not ruled the island of Taiwan, Beijing has claimed that Taiwan is a part of China and should be "reunified" either peacefully or through the use of force if necessary. Beijing sees as its right a military option for resolving the dispute. It underlines this point with large scale military exercises near Taiwan. Beijing used unusually public military exercises, including unprecedented missile launches, near Taiwan in 1995 as a means to intimidate Taiwan from pursuing a more independent role in world affairs, notably by sending senior Taiwan leaders to the U.S.

Regarding Hong Kong, on September 23, 1993, China published Deng Xiaoping's statement to British Prime Minister Margaret Thatcher in 1982. Chinese publications quoted Deng's warning that China would "reconsider the timing and manner of the takeover," if there were serious "disturbances" in Hong Kong during the transition to change in sovereignty.[37]

PLA modernization is also intended to secure Chinese economic interests in offshore resources. The South China Sea is believed to hold oil and gas potential, although substantial exploration still needs to be completed. In 1992, Vice Admi-

[34]See among others, CRS Report 95-46S.

[35]See, for example, *East Asia: Disputed Islands and Offshore Claims -- Issues for U.S. Policy*, CRS Report 92-614S, by Robert Sutter, July 28, 1992.

[36]Washington does not side with any claimant, but wants a peaceful resolution of the dispute and freedom of navigation in the South China Sea. See CRS Report 92-614S, *op. cit.*

[37]Xinhua News Agency, September 23, 1993.

ral Zhang Xusan of the PLA Navy stated "it is high time for China to readjust its maritime strategy and make more efforts to recover the oil and gas resources in the South China Sea."[38]

Willingness to Use Force

Since its founding in October 1949, the PRC has opted to use armed force in a number of disputes, rather than pursue a peaceful, negotiated settlement. Examples include:

- Takeover of Tibet (October 1950-October 1951): After the civil war against Republic of China forces on the Chinese mainland, the PLA expanded its control to Tibetan areas and has since maintained control;[39]
- Korean War (1950-53): The PLA entered the Korean War in October 1950 to support North Korean troops against the U.N. forces led by the United States;[40]
- Taiwan Strait Crisis (1954-55): The PLA in September 1954 launched heavy artillery attacks on the offshore island of Quemoy and in November, PLA plumes bombed and subsequently occupied the Tachen Islands. The United States signed the Mutual Defense Treaty with the Nationalist government on Taiwan on December 2, 1954;[41]
- Second Taiwan Strait Crisis (1958): The PLA engaged in artillery attacks on two offshore islands (Quemoy and Matsu) held by the Nationalists and threatened American naval ships;[42]
- Sino-Indian Border War (1962): In October 1962, the PLA launched attacks on two disputed areas along the Sino-Indian eastern and western borders. In the west, the PLA expanded its line of control to include the Aksai Chin, considered strategically important to China because Chinese workers had built a road through the area to connect western Tibet with Xinjiang;[43]
- Vietnam War (1964-70): When the U.S. escalated military action in 1964, the PLA, among other support, deployed warplanes and large numbers of troops in North Vietnam, conducted joint air exercises with the North Vietnamese, launched antiaircraft artillery on American planes, provided

[38] *China Daily*, April 6, 1992, p. 4.

[39] See among others, *A History of Modern Tibet, 1913-1951*, by Melvyn C. Goldstein, University of California Press, 1989.

[40] See Allen S. Whiting, *China Crosses the Yalu*, Stanford University Press, 1960, and Harlan W. Jencks, *From Muskets to Missiles: Politics and Professionalism in the Chinese Army, 1945-1981*, Westview Press, 1982.

[41] See among others, Roderick MacFarquhar, *Sino-American Relations, 1949-71*, Praeger Publishers, 1972.

[42] *Ibid.*

[43] Gerard H. Corr, *The Chinese Red Army: Campaigns and Politics since 1949*, Schocken Books, 1974; and Neville Maxwell, *India's China War*, Jonathan Cape Limited, 1970.

direct military aid, and protected North Vietnamese troops and warplanes along the Sino-Vietnamese border;[44]

- Sino-Soviet Border Clash (1969): The soviet Union and China clashed in the disputed Amur-Ussuri border area in March 1969, after PLA troops intruded to stake their claim on Damansky/Chen Pao Island;[45]
- Paracel Islands (1974): In 1974, the PLA took control of several disputed Paracel Islands in the South China Sea by forcefully ousting South Vietnamese forces which had occupied the islands for many years. The PLA takeover occurred before North Vietnam could occupy the Paracels after the country's unification in 1975;[46]
- Sino-Vietnam Border War (1979): In February 1979, after failing to deter Vietnam's invasion of Cambodia, China dispatched the PLA in a limited, one-month invasion of Vietnam, "to teach Vietnam a lesson;"[47]
- Sino-Indian Border Skirmishes (1986-87): In 1986, India reported that PLA troops intruded into Indian territory beyond the line of control established at the end of the 1962 war. In talks with U.S. Defense Secretary Weinberger in October 1986, Deng Xiaoping threatened to "teach India a lesson" if India did not stop "nibbling" at Chinese territory;[48]
- Spratly Islands (1988): In March 1988, the PLA forcefully ousted Vietnamese forces and took control of some islets in the Spratlys.[49]
- Taiwan (1995): In reaction to the Taiwan President's June 1995 visit to the U.S., Beijing initiated large scale military exercises, including provocative missile launches, and a steady stream of harsh rhetoric threatening Taiwan and its leaders.

---

[44] Robert S. Ross, *The Indochina Tangle: China's Vietnam Policy 1975-1979*, Columbia University Press, 1980; and Harlan W. Jencks (1982).

[45] See Corr (1974).

[46] See Ross (1988); and Robert G. Sutter, *East Asia: Disputed Islands and Offshore Claims–Issues for U.S. Policy*, CRS Report, July 28, 1992.

[47] Ross (1988).

[48] David Bonavia, "Troubled Frontiers," *Far Eastern Economic Review*, September 4, 1986, p. 14-15; Nayan Chanda, "Heading for a Conflict," *Far Eastern Economic Review*, June 4, 1987, p. 42-43; and Robert G. Sutter and Richard P. Cronin, *China-India Border Friction: Background Information and Possible Implications*, CRS Report, June 19, 1987.

[49] Jerry Cushing, "Beached Again on Shoals," *Far Eastern Economic Review*, March 17, 1988, p. 23-25; *Far Eastern Economic Review*, March 24, 1988, p. 10, and August 13, 1992, p. 15.

Factors Arguing Against Viewing China as a Current or Emerging Threat

Capabilities

Despite the recent buildup, many analysts tend to view the PLA as a demonstrably backward force. It is depicted as trying not to fall further behind the more advanced technological abilities of China's neighbors, while facing a political situation at home that still emphasizes economic modernization over defense spending.

The roots of China's defense backwardness go deep into the Maoist period and the prolonged confrontation with the Soviet Union. At that time (1960s-1980s), China's defense depended on a military strategy heavily reliant on ground forces that expected to engage the invading enemy on Chinese territory. China gave special attention to the development of a reliable nuclear counterattack capability, mainly through mobile nuclear-tipped missiles, to deter the Soviets from using nuclear weapons against China. Apart from such missiles, the PLA's ability to project power beyond its borders remained limited. The Navy and Air Force were weak in power projection, remaining focused respectively on coastal defense and air interdiction of intruding enemy forces.[50]

Weakness in power projection were graphically illustrated during China's military incursion into northern parts of Vietnam in early 1979.[51] The incursion was designed to "punish" Hanoi for invading Cambodia the previous December and to divert Vietnamese military attention from possible expansion against Thailand or elsewhere in Southeast Asia. The Chinese succeeded in diverting few Vietnamese main force units. The PLA had to contend with the well seasoned Vietnamese militia forces in the region.

Beijing's biggest obstacle turned out to be the PLA's cumbersome force structure, obsolete strategy, and outdated weapons. Although enjoying a large numerical superiority over the smaller Vietnamese air force, the Chinese chose not to employ air power to assist the advance. Western analysts suspected the reason was Beijing's inexperience in combined arms operations, along with a fear of losing many expensive aircraft to Vietnamese ground fire and fighter aircraft. The resulting Chinese assault took on features of the plodding artillery-infantry advances seen along the Eastern and Western fronts during World War I. The Vietnamese militia acquitted themselves well, holding and then slowly withdrawing from local strong points and imposing heavy casualties on the Chinese

---

[50]For useful overviews of Chinese military developments during this period, see the military chapters in the U.S. Congress. Joint Economic Committee, "China Under the Four Modernization," 1982; "China's Economy Looks Toward the Year 2000," 1986; and "China's Economic Dilemmas in the 1990s," 1991.

[51]See sources cited in footnote 48. See also relevant discussion in CRS Report 95-46S.

invaders. When PLA forces withdrew after one month of operations, their casualties were in the range of 30,000.[52]

Chinese planners endeavored to learn from the Vietnamese experience. A major realignment of China's military strategy begun in the mid-1980s shifted the PLA away from past emphasis on a major war with the USSR and placed more emphasis on mobile warfare, combined arms operations and more modern military equipment. But defense budgets and defense spending were on the decline throughout the decade. The U.S. Arms Control and Disarmament Agency estimated that actual Chinese defense spending in 1989 was 25 percent less than actual Chinese defense spending in 1979.[53]

Chinese procurement specialists tried to put their limited budgets to good use. Extensive lists were drawn up by PLA leaders anxious to acquire more advanced weapons systems useful for the type of smaller scale warfare and power projection needs anticipated by Chinese leaders. Nonetheless few deals were actually made, and those that were made often involved the upgrading of existing Chinese platforms (planes, ships, tanks, etc.) with more advanced avionics, fire control systems, guns, etc.

Several of these arrangements did not work as planned. For example, having purchased British "Spey" engines for use in the Chinese derivative of the MIG 21 fighter--the mainstay of China's air defense--Chinese officials eventually decided to abandon plans to incorporate the foreign power plant. This costly failure appeared to demonstrate that Beijing still had not worked out the defects in the Chinese MIG 21 engine which have made Chinese reluctant to use the planes extensively, in part for fear of rapid engine burnout. Meanwhile, the Chinese plan to upgrade the F-8 jet interceptor with U.S. technology was thrown over by U.S. sanctions on such military sales after the 1989 Tiananmen crackdown, leading to cancellation of the project.

What upgrades and purchases have taken place or are planned often show little sign of substantially improving Chinese military capabilities, especially in sensitive areas of power projection. Notable continuing Chinese limitations include:[54]

- A large (100) submarine force with very dated boats (as many as one half may no longer be operational); difficulty in communications adds to reasons for keeping boats close to shore. China's record of fatal sub accidents is among the worst in the world, especially given the limited amount of time such boats actually spend at sea;

---

[52] See John Garver, Foreign Relations of the People's of China, Prentice Hall, Englewood Cliffs, N.J., 1993, p. 315.

[53] U.S. Arms Control and Disarmament Agency, World Military Expenditures and Arms Transfers, 1990, Table I.

[54] Details of China's Force Structure are listed in *The Military Balance*, IISS, London, (annual).

- A large (5,000) jet fighter- and bomber-force based--at best--on early 1960s Soviet derivatives that are often mechanically unreliable and therefore are restricted in use.
- A decades-long Chinese search for a reliable air refueling system that would extend the very limited range of Chinese aircraft;
- Infrequency of live-fire exercises and other activities that prepare the armed forces for actual combat.
- Continued weak command and control systems--this argues for caution in deploying forces far from headquarters;
- Relatively few transport helicopters to assist force mobility; continued reliance of World War II type land and sea-based movement for deployment of troops.

The lessons of the Persian Gulf war 1991-1992 were seen to underline China's relatively weak capabilities in critical areas. The ability of well trained Western forces armed with high-technology weaponry to conduct effective combined arms operations against Iraqi forces showed Beijing how far behind it actually was in dealing with modern warfare. Beijing leaders were well aware that Chinese forces would continue to have much more in common with those of Saddam Hussein than with the West. It is clear as well that the forces deployed around China's eastern periphery (especially those of Japan, South Korea, and Taiwan) and to a lesser degree some forces in Southeast Asia (notably Singapore) have the kind of fire power, mobility, training, and experience that the allies used to successfully against Iraq.

Although Chinese defense budgets began to go up to help redress some of the problems in capabilities, Chinese defense spending has been somewhat negatively affected by the drop off in Chinese arms sales abroad in recent years. The decline in sales stemmed from the loss of the Iran-Iraq market following the termination of that war, and the desire of most foreign buyers to obtain equipment more advanced than that sold by China.[55]

Chinese military capabilities also have suffered in a relative sense because many of China's neighbors--especially to the East and south--continue to outface China in terms of defense technology, modernization and relative defense spending:[56]

---

[55]See, *Conventional Arms Transfers to the Third World*, 1985-1992, Richard Grimmett, CRS Report 93-656F, July 19, 1993, 84 p.

[56]See among others, Michael Klare, "The Next Great Arms Race," *Foreign Affairs*, summer 1993; Hu Weixing, "Economic Growth, Defense Industries, and Armament Dynamic: Interpreting the Military Building in East Asia, conference paper, May 1993; Wang Qi, "The Chinese Perspective on Multilateral Security Arrangements in the Asia-Pacific Region," conference paper, May 1993; Michael Gallagher, "China's Illusory Threat to the South China Sea," *International Security*, summer 1994.

- Throughout the 1980's, Japan, South Korea and Taiwan all experienced continuous increases in military spending, at a rate of 4-5 percent a year. China's military spending steadily declined in the same period.[57]
- In the 1980s, most East Asian countries began to incorporate sophisticated weapons more capable of power projection into their armed forces. Japan and South Korea moved this way first, in the late 1970s and early 1980s, followed by Taiwan, Singapore, Malaysia and Indonesia. In this respect, China's recent upgrading can be seen as that of a laggard trying to catch up. A few examples include:
  - Japan's AEGIS destroyers, new submarines and air refueling tankers all designed to help defend sea lines of communication to 1,000 miles around Japan;
  - Taiwan's acquisitions of F-16 and Mirage fighters, French and American advanced frigates and new U.S. air defense systems;
  - South Korea's acquisition of F-16 fighters, new submarines, frigates and helicopters.

All ASEAN states, with the exception of the Philippines, have been upgrading naval and air force capabilities related to their switch from past focus on home/coastal defense to current emphasis on providing a greater range of striking power and force projection. All, except Malaysia and Brunei, have purchased F-16 aircraft and moved to phase out current F-5 fighters. Malaysia purchased a few F-18s along with some MIG 29s from Russia. In naval capabilities, Indonesia has purchased 6 Van Speijk-class frigates, Malaysia is buying two sophisticated frigates from Britain, while Thailand has commissioned two Chinese-built frigates. Singapore has fitted six of its 24 fast-attack craft with Harpoon surface-to-surface missiles.

Intentions

Although aspirations to greater power and military superiority may dominate some of the private thoughts and public pronouncements of certain Chinese leaders, including members of the PLA high command, the fact remains that Chinese leaders continue to face a number of considerations that offset or moderate any expansionist intent. Heading the list is the logic which has dominated Chinese international security and foreign policies in the post-Mao period:[58]

---

[57] U.S. Arms Control and Disarmamemt Agency, World Military Expenditure and Arms Transfers, 1990, Table I.

[58] For background, see among others, *China in World Affairs--Background, Prospects and Implications for the U.S.*, by Robert Sutter, CRS Report 92-747S, October 1, 1992, 28 p.

- Post-Mao Chinese communist leaders need to foster a better economic life for the people of China in order to legitimate and justify their continued monopoly of power. These leaders cannot rely as Mao did on his enormous personal prestige as a successful revolutionary, or on the attractiveness of Communist ideology: they have little of Mao's prestige, and the attractiveness of Communist ideology is largely a thing of the past.
- China depends critically on foreign trade, and related foreign investment and assistance, for its economic development.
- China depends particularly heavily on its neighbors for aid, investment, and trade benefits, and on the United States to absorb its exports.
- Therefore, to insure their survival politically, post-Mao leaders emphasize their concern with maintaining a "peaceful" international environment which assures continued trade, investment, and assistance flows so important to Chinese economic well being.

The bottom line as far as China's international security and foreign policies are concerned is that Chinese leaders are not inclined to confront those countries so important to China's economic modernization. A case in point relates to Chinese policy toward the United States since the Tiananmen incident. Despite what Beijing views as repeated American affronts and insults to the Chinese Communist regime, the Chinese government sees its interests best served by continuing to seek common ground with the U.S. on economic and security issues. This reasoning helped to explain China's willingness to resume dialogue with the Clinton Administration following its outburst of harsh rhetoric over the Taiwan President's visit to the U.S. in June 1995.[59] The same reasoning holds true for China's relations with Japan and other Asian neighbors, although they, for their own reasons, have been less likely than the U.S. to take action directly antagonistic to the PRC.

The Chinese also need to restrain any expansionist intent because their neighbors, backed by the United States, have become particularly vigilant in monitoring Chinese military moves. Some Chinese neighbors have called for countermeasures. Over the past few years, Chinese leaders have reacted defensively to media and official charges in the region and the West about China's emerging military threat. They have gone to considerable lengths in high level meetings and visits to the East Asian region to reassure those concerned with China's intentions, especially regarding the disputed islands in the South China Sea. Chinese officials express worry publicly and privately that critics in the region and the West will use recent interest in Asian regional security arrangements to set up an international alignment directed at the Chinese threat.

[59] See CRS Issue Brief 94002.

ASSESSMENT

Factors arguing in favor of and against viewing China as a military threat show that the main danger to U.S. interests over the next few years focuses on areas in the Asian-Pacific region around China's periphery where China and other countries important to the U.S. contest territorial claims. (China's current military capabilities generally show little sign of China's posing a direct threat to the United States for a decade or longer.)[60]

Perceived Chinese expansionist designs to control contested areas which China claims around its periphery are currently held in check by limitations in PLA capabilities; insufficient justification in terms of important Chinese security, economic or political interests; and the likely negative foreign reaction to an assertive Chinese action.

Each of these factors is subject to change. An important case in point for the United States involves Taiwan, an area of long-standing importance for U.S. economic, political and security interests. For many years, PRC leaders have seen little to be gained in resorting to force in order to assert their claim to the island. They have repeatedly warned, however, that Beijing would not hesitate to use force in response to changed conditions, such as a challenge to China's claimed sovereignty posed by a formal Taiwan declaration of independence. In the past, the ruling Nationalist Party in Taiwan strongly adhered to a "one-China" policy and ruled in an authoritarian fashion against advocates of Taiwan independence. Political democratization in Taiwan in recent years has seen a weakening of Nationalist Party rule and the rise of a growing political opposition formally dedicated to seeking Taiwan independence. Circumstances could arise in the not-too-distant future where a government in Taiwan might in declare independence--a formal challenge to Beijing's claim of sovereignty that in turn might greatly increase the likelihood of forceful military action (e.g., blockade) against the island.[61] Indeed, PRC military exercises and rhetorical threats to use force were directed at Taiwan following Taiwan President Lee Teng-hui's June 1995 visit to the United States. They appeared designed to intimidate perceived pro-independence advocates on Taiwan.

Also of current concern to observers in Asia and the West is the potential for further Chinese expansion in disputed areas of the South China Sea. Most notably, China, Taiwan and Vietnam claim the entire collection of islets and reefs known as the Spratly Islands, while Malaysia and the Philippines have claims to parts of the territory. All the countries maintain armed forced on some of the

---

[60] In general, U.S. experts see PLA leaders as having learned a lot in recent years about developing a truly modern military force capable of projecting significant power beyond China's borders. Thus, some say, the PLA "knows what to do" to develop this kind of power and the PLA "knows how to do it." The questions that remain are whether the PLA will be able to or want to do it.

[61] The current and prospective military balance in the Taiwan Strait argues against direct PRC assault on the island--Taiwan's defenses are strong. A blockade, relying on Beijing's superiority in submarines, is seen as more likely. See among others Parris Chang and Martin Lasater, *If China Crosses the Taiwan Strait*, University Press of America, 1993. See also CRS Report 95-968S.

islets. At present, the PLA has sufficient military capabilities to expand its territorial holdings, especially in areas currently held or claimed by Vietnam. Beijing continues methodically to increase capabilities (e.g., building airstrips) that would allow China to deploy forces sufficient to establish air and sea control around disputed islets or reefs. A strategic rationale for Chinese actions is provided by the fact that the region is located along sea lines of communications of importance to China. It may contain important oil and gas reserves useful for China's economic modernization, which a successful military operation to assert Chinese nationalistic claims would presumably redound to the domestic political benefit of leaders in Beijing.[62]

The main deterrent to Chinese expansion at present appears to be Chinese leaders' concern with foreign reaction. Assertive Chinese claims, aggressive military patrolling, provocative oil exploration, and other activities have generated substantial negative foreign reaction from time to time.

China has been concerned to avoid direct U.S. intervention in these disputes. U.S. interests are less directly involved in this area than in Taiwan, but U.S. leaders in the Bush and Clinton Administrations have emphasized American interests in the peaceful resolution of these problems. Recent action included a May 10, 1995 State Department statement on the South China sea and a November 29, 1995 State Department statement on Taiwan.[63] The implication is left that the U.S. might take unspecified actions against those (mainly China) seen to be taking assertive actions threatening peace in the region.

Indicators of Chinese Military Threat

Several variables or indicators govern the likelihood of more or less assertive Chinese behavior threatening to U.S. interests in peace and stability in the Asian-Pacific Region.

Indicators of Increased Prospects of Threatening Chinese Behavior

- Emergence of a power vacuum in the Asia-Pacific Region. This could provide a greater incentive for Chinese military expansion and reduce negative consequences that might flow from such expansion.
- Sharp increase in national assertiveness by PRC leaders. This could result from a Chinese leadership power struggle. For example, an ascendant faction might endeavor to use strident nationalistic rhetoric and military actions in order to rally domestic political support.

[62]See review of this controversy in *East Asia: Disputed Island and Offshore Claims--Issues for U.S. Policy*, Robert Sutter, CRS Report 92-614S, July 28, 1992, 15 p.

[63]See CRS issue briefs 93114 and 94006.

-- Broad, successful technological modernization of the PLA. A marked increase in PLA capabilities to project power, especially air and naval power, relative to other states in the region would dramatically increase the range of actions Chinese leaders might take in order to assert their nationalistic, territorial claims.

-- Less Chinese dependence on/concern over Asian-Pacific, Western countries. This could come about due to economic success in China. Such success could cause Asian-Pacific and Western countries to judge that they need to cater to China despite Beijing's military threats. Alternatively, if Asian-Pacific and Western countries were to decide to isolate China (e.g., U.S. withdraw MFN trade privileges), they could force Beijing into a more autarchic development strategy that reduces China's dependence on economic ties with the outside world and China's concern with international reaction to Chinese military expansion.

-- Actions by groups or leaders around China's periphery seen as challenging fundamental interests of the Chinese state. This could include a Taiwan declaration of independence; substantial Indian support--military equipment, training--for armed Tibetan resistance to Chinese rule; or other possibilities.

Indicators of Reduced Prospects of Threatening Chinese Behavior

-- Continued Chinese leadership preoccupation with domestic economic, political and social problems. This could give little opportunity to divert resources to controversial expansionist actions.

-- Growing Chinese economic interdependence with Asian-Pacific, Western countries. Dependent on economic modernization for political success, Chinese leaders presumably could not afford to alienate these important sources of economic support.

-- Continued PLA backwardness relative to likely adversaries. This could reinforce caution of PRC leaders, avoiding use of forces where they might be defeated or cause such losses as to embarrass and undermine support for the regime.

-- Strengthened regional efforts to deal with China. On the one hand, this could involve military buildups by countries in the region along with the U.S., and the establishment of multilateral arrangements to put pressure on the Chinese to avoid provocative or disruptive actions. On the other hand, regional arrangements could be designed to include and "engage" the Chinese in s series of mutually supporting discussions and activities. These in turn presumably would persuade the PRC leaders that they had more to gain from working constructively with others concerned with peace and security in the region than by adopting threatening measures upsetting to peace and stability.

U.S. Policy Implications, Role of the U.S. and U.S. Policy Choices

U.S. Policy Implications

While it may appear easy to exaggerate the threat posed by the PLA to U.S. interests, it is no exaggeration to point out the PLA's multifaceted importance for the future of China. In this way, policy directions and actions by the PLA can have important implications for the United States. The U.S. has significant interests in each of the four issue areas examined in this report, and the PLA affects each of those issue areas. For example:

- More PLA influence in the PRC central leadership could reduce the amount of local autonomy available to provincial and other local leaders. This in turn could reduce the slowly developing trends toward political pluralism in China, perpetuating a central authoritarian regime following political policies contrary to U.S. values and ideals.
- If the PLA gains more influence, it may gain a freer hand in dealing with internal security issues, possibly prompting a harder PRC line against dissident, national minority agitators, and others in China pressing for greater individual and civil rights in accord with U.S. interests.
- Increases in the defense budgets and other allocations for the PLA will affect domestic spending in China and in turn affect foreign businesses, including those from the U.S. anxious to do business in China. PLA resource allocation could slow the pace of reform away from the state enterprises system and affect the balance between heavy and light industry in China -- both features important in determining the economic atmosphere and opportunities for foreign businesses dealing with China.
- The PLA has a direct bearing on U.S. security concerns regarding proliferation, nuclear testing, military spending and sensitive territorial issues along China's periphery which have a direct bearing on U.S. interest in continued peace and stability in Asia and the Pacific and in world affairs generally.

Role of the U.S.[64]

Although the United States does not border on China, Beijing leaders, including PLA leaders. recognize that the United States exerts predominant strategic influence in East Asia and the Western Pacific; is a leading economic power in the region, surpassed locally only by Japan; and is one of only two world powers capable of exerting sufficient power around China's periphery to pose a tangible danger to Chinese security and development. As the world's only superpower, the United States also exerts strong influence in international financial and political institutions (e.g., the World Bank and the UN) that are very important to Beijing, and the U.S. role in particular areas sensitive to Beijing, notably policy regarding Taiwan and international human rights, is second to none.[65]

The pattern of international interchange with China's growing strength in recent years appears to underline the importance of the U.S. role. Few of China's neighbors are willing to challenge or express strongly different views from the PRC on major issues. They privately support a significant U.S. military presence in the region, partly because it serves as an implicit counterweight to China's military power. They and more distant developed countries also privately support firm U.S. efforts to open China's markets, end unfair commercial practices, and protect the integrity of the world trading system. And they appreciate the U.S. efforts to press China to end nuclear testing and proliferation of equipment and technology for weapons of mass destruction.[66] Notably, however, this support is usually not expressed openly.

Beijing leaders, including PLA commanders, also see the United States as the key link in the international balance of power affecting Chinese interests. This judgment goes far toward explaining why Chinese leaders have sought U.S.-china summit meetings. They view such meetings as signaling to those at home and abroad that the United States has muffled its opposition to and endorses cooperation with the Beijing government. Of course, some Chinese leaders, including some in the PLA, remain deeply suspicious of U.S. motives. They believe the U.S. government is conspiring to weaken and undermine the Chinese leadership and "hold back" China from a more prominent position in world affairs.[67]

In general, Chinese leaders, including those in the PLA, do not see the United States as a strategic enemy that is likely to attack or otherwise take military action against China. Rather, Chinese leaders suspicious of U.S. motives tend to see a pattern in U.S. diplomatic, economic, and other interaction with China that

---

[64] For further discussion see CRS Reports 95-265S and 95-46S.

[65] See, CRS Report 95-265S. It is worth noting that recent internal PRC studies have concluded that the United States will continue to be the world's only superpower at least through the year 2010. Interviews, November 13, 1995.

[66] Ibid.

[67] See, among others, *Sino-U.S. Relations: Status and Outlook--Views from Beijing*, CRS memorandum, August 15, 1994.

appears designed to hamper the development of China's power. U.S. support for a Taiwan separate from PRC control is a recent case in point, but other examples include U.S. support for political dissidents in China, firm U.S. demands of China regarding intellectual property rights and market access prior to U.S. acquiescence in China's entry into the World Trade Organization (WTO), and U.S. support for Tibetan Autonomy from PRC dominance.

Such suspicions do not preclude PLA leaders from seeking closer interaction and engagement with the United States, especially U.S. military leaders. On the one hand, Chinese military leaders are like their U.S. counterparts in seeking such bilateral exchanges in order to understand one another better and in so doing to be better prepared to deal with contingencies, especially negative ones. In effect, both sides are using engagement as a "hedge" against possible adverse changes in the relationship.

On the other hand, Chinese military leaders also hope to achieve a number of more specific benefits from interaction with U.S. counterparts including:

- Knowledge taken from the experience of U.S. forces, clearly seen by the PLA as the dominant military forces in the world for the foreseeable future.
- Possible access to U.S. technology, and perhaps some dual use or other equipment, that could prove useful in China's military modernization.
- More influence on U.S. decisions pertaining to U.S. arms sales to Taiwan.
- Establishment of procedures to avoid incidents that occur when PLA and U.S. forces face each other at close range in East Asia.
- Prestige both at home and abroad that comes from close association with the world's premier military force.
- Constructive interaction with the United States designed to support a security environment in East Asia that does not pose serious problems for China's goals of modernization. This involves in particular encouraging U.S. policies in Japan and Korea that enhance China's security, along with U.S. military activities in southeast Asia that meet China's needs. In general, Beijing supports a moderate U.S. stance toward the North Korean military threat, a continued U.S. military presence in Japan that would dampen possible Japanese military expansion, and a low profile for U.S. forces in Southeast Asia.

There is general agreement in the United States that Washington should use its influence in order to have Beijing conform to international norms and over time to foster changes in China's political, economic, and security systems compatible with American interests. At the same time, there is little agreement in Washington on how the United States should achieve these objectives. In general, there appear to be three approaches influencing current U.S. China policy and little indication as to which approach will ultimately succeed.[68]

On one side is an approach favored by some in the Clinton Administration, the Congress and elsewhere who argue in favor of a moderate, less confrontational, and more "engaged" posture toward China. Some in this camp are concerned with perceived fundamental weaknesses in China and urge a moderate U.S. policy approach out of fear that to do otherwise could promote divisions in and a possible breakup of China with potentially disastrous consequences for U.S. interests in Asian stability and prosperity. Others are more impressed with China's growing economic and national strength and the opportunities this provides for the United States. They promote closer U.S. engagement with China as the most appropriate way to guide the newly emerging power into channels f international activity compatible with American interests.

Sometimes underlying this moderate approach is a belief that trends in China are moving inexorably in the "right" direction. That is, China is becoming increasingly interdependent economically with its neighbors and the developed countries of the West, and is seen as increasingly unlikely to take disruptive action that would upset these advantageous international economic relationships. In addition, greater wealth in China is seen pushing Chinese society in directions that seem certain to develop a materially better-off, more educated and cosmopolitan populace that will over time press its government for greater representation, political pluralism and eventually democracy. Therefore, U.S. policy should seek to work ever more closely with China in order to encourage these positive long term trends.

A second, tougher approach is that of some U.S. advocates inside and out of the U.S. Government who have doubts about the interdependence argument. These U.S. policymakers and opinion leaders stress that Beijing officials still view the world as a state-centered competitive environment where interdependence counts for little and compromises sovereign strength. China's leaders are seen as determined to use whatever means at their disposal to increase China's wealth and power. At present, Beijing is seen biding its time and conforming to many international norms as it builds economic strength. Once it succeeds with economic modernization, the argument goes, Beijing will be disinclined to curb its narrow nationalistic or other ambitions out of a need for international interdependence of other concerns for world community. when strong enough, China, like other large powers in the past, will possess great capabilities and will attract no few friends or allies.

Under these circumstances, this approach encourages U.S. leaders to be more firm than moderate in dealing with China. Rather than trying to persuade Beijing of the advantages of international cooperation, the United States is advised to keep military forces as a counterweight to rising Chinese power in Asia; to

[68]Reviewed in CRS Report 95-265S.

remain firm in dealing with economic, arms proliferation and other disputes with China; and to work closely with traditional U.S. allies and friends along China's periphery in order to deal with any suspected assertiveness or disruption from Beijing.

A third approach is favored by some U.S. officials and others who believe that the political system in China needs to be changed before the United States has any real hope of reaching a constructive relationship with China. Beijing's communist leaders are seen as inherently incapable of long term positive ties with the United States. U.S. policy should focus on mechanisms to change China from within while maintaining a vigilant posture to deal with disruptive Chinese foreign policy actions in Asian and world affairs. The development of an authoritarian superpower more economically competent than the USSR is not to be aided.

The Clinton Administration military leaders recently have endeavored to portray their "engagement" policy toward the PLA as containing elements of the first and second approaches. In a speech on October 30, 1995, Secretary of Defense William Perry said that the Administration's "comprehensive engagement" with China will help the two countries to "work together where we agree and reduce tensions where we disagree," and will allow the United States to "reinforce positive developments in China and encourage China to become a stabilizing influence in the region and in the world." Perry went on to assert that "engagement does not equal appeasement or even accommodation," adding that the U.S. Government is "committed to engagement, but not at any price."[69]

U.S. Policy Options

U.S. policymakers have a range of unilateral, bilateral and multilateral options for dealing with China's military power. They include positive and negative incentives designed to influence Chinese behavior in ways that enhance regional stability and curb China's potential expansion.

Unilateral. The U.S. military presence in Asia helps to maintain stability in the region and avoids the creation of a power vacuum that Beijing might be tempted to fill. There is disagreement in the U.S. over the size and scope of this presence, especially given competing U.S. spending priorities and Asian allies ability to provide more for their own defense. Pentagon plans call for retaining almost 100,000 troops in Asia, based mainly in South Korea and Japan. The U.S. military presence also solidifies U.S. relations with key Asian states (e.g., Japan, Korea) and encourages them to continue to side with the U.S. in the event of serious differences with China over regional security issues.

U.S. arms sales to Asian countries also reassure allies and friends of U.S. resolve and reinforce stability. On the other hand, they are seen as fueling arms races in sensitive areas. In particular, some believe that the U.S. sales of 150 F-16

[69] Speech by Secretary of Defense William Perry, Seattle, Washington, October 30, 1995.

fighters to Taiwan may provoke a PRC counter effort that will exacerbate tensions and add to regional instability. Others, of course, see the sales as needed to reassure friends in Taiwan faced with rising PRC air power.

Bilateral. Positive U.S. incentives include the recent efforts of the Clinton Administration to broaden and heighten U.S. official dialogue with Chinese leaders, including those of the PLA. Through such dialogues, seen notable in Defense Secretary William Perry's October 1994 visit to China, both sides are presumably reassured regarding the military-security actions and intentions of the other, and are less inclined to take drastic action in response. The overall effect is thought to be calming and stabilizing for the Asian-Pacific region.

U.S. engagement with China also involves interaction in political, economic and other areas that are assumed to make Chinese policymakers more supportive of the international status quo and less prone to disruptive action in Asian and world affairs.

Negative U.S. incentives stem logically from the positive ones. The U.S. has the option to cut back ties important to PRC leaders in response to perceived provocative or threatening Chinese action. Areas most sensitive to China are economic ties, especially access to the U.S. market determined annually by the President with the concurrence of Congress regarding whether or not to grant Most-Favored-Nation trade treatment to Chinese imports to the U.S. China is also keenly interested in U.S. investment and high technology; U.S. policymakers have levers to regulate the flow of such benefits depending in part on Chinese policy and actions in the Asian-Pacific region.

Multilateral. On the positive side, the United States could work more actively with China and other regional powers to reach security arrangements that reassured all parties and enhanced stability. Because of its unique role as the region's only superpower and its perceived importance for all major Asian powers (e.g., Japan, China, Russia), the United States can play a catalytic role more effectively than others. Such multilateral engagement with China would presumably have the objective of demonstrating to PRC leaders that their concerns about the intentions of others have been exaggerated and that China has more to gain from a continued cooperative approach toward the region. Forums that might be used in this endeavor include the annual Association of Southeast Asian Nations' (ASEAN) Post-Ministerial dialogue involving most powers in the region. Some suggest the economic forum, Asian-Pacific Economic Cooperation (APEC), which includes more countries, might evolve into a forum useful for regional security questions. Most promising recently have been the meetings of the so-called ASEAN Regional Forum -- an annual security dialogue among countries in East Asia.

The United States also has the option to work with other countries to restrain or check suspected Chinese expansion. The United States has considerable influence with Russia, Israel, and European countries and could encourage them to curb sales of sensitive equipment to China. Multilateral export controls could be used to curb sensitive sales to China. U.S. allies and long-standing friends along the periphery of Asia also could be expected to work closely with the United States in the event that China challenged regional stability with expansionist military activity in the South China Sea or elsewhere. In particular, China remains heavily dependent on aid from Japan and from international financial institutions led by Japan and the U.S. Adroit use of this aid could provide the allies with powerful leverage in dissuading Chinese leaders from military assertiveness.

OUTLOOK FOR U.S. POLICY

Given the continued wide range of opinion in the United States over the appropriate U.S. policy toward China, it appears likely that U.S. policy will continue its recent pattern of trying to accommodate elements of the three approaches discussed on pages 35-37. On some issues, like linking MFN treatment and human rights, the U.S. Government has seen U.S. interests best served by an approach that meets PRC concerns. On others, like intellectual property rights protection and proliferation of missile technology, the United States Government seems prepared to threaten sanctions or to withhold benefits from Beijing until it conforms to norms acceptable to the United States. Meanwhile, although many U.S. officials would see as counterproductive any declaration by the U.S. Government that a policy goal was to change China's system of government, there is a widespread assumption that greater U.S. "engagement" will encourage such desirable changes.

Whether the U.S. Government synthesis of these three tendencies is done smoothly or is accompanied by the often strident policy debates accompanying U.S. China policy decisions in recent years depends partly on U.S. leadership. In this vein, specialists interviewed for this report suggested several rules of thumb that U.S. leaders could consider when determining whether the United States should try to accommodate, confront or change China on a particular policy issue:

1. How important is the issue at hand for U.S. interests? (In general the more important the U.S. interests at stake, the less accommodating and more forceful U.S. leaders should be.)
2. How does the issue at hand fit in with broader U.S. strategic interests in relation with China? (Presumably, some U.S. officials would be inclined to soft pedal relatively minor disputes with China when they are pressing for broader gains elsewhere.)
3. How much leverage does the United States have over the PRC on this issue? (In general, the greater the degree of U.S. leverage, the easier it is for U.S. leaders to press for their demands.)

4. What are the attitudes of U.S. allies and associates? (If they do not support a firm U.S. stance, U.S. efforts to pressure China may be outflanked, Quixotic or counterproductive.)
5. How sensitive is the issue at hand to the PRC. (Experience has indicated that Beijing has shown less sensitivity and greater flexibility on international economic issues, and has shown more sensitivity and less flexibility on issues involving domestic political control and territorial claims. Many analysts believe that PRC leadership flexibility on sensitive issues will be restricted for a time as a result of the decline of Deng Xiaoping's health and the ongoing leadership succession struggle.)

Other matters of importance in considering specific Chin policy issues include:

- How does the U.S. stance affect broader U.S. interests in Asian stability and international affairs?
- What is the U.S. "bottom line?" Chinese officials will press for the advantage until they find it.
- Can this matter be effectively pursued in an overall friendly and respectful atmosphere? Doing so reduces suspicions in Beijing regarding the alleged overall hostile intent of U.S. policymakers toward China -- suspicions which greatly limit PRC flexibility.
- Can this issue be pursued with the aid of U.S. allies, associates and other international leaders to create an atmosphere that would prompt Beijing to change in directions favored by the United States? (The United States used this approach in part to bet Beijing to go along with international sanctions and military action against Libya and Iraq; with planned sanctions against North Korea; and with provisions of the 1991 Cambodian peace accord that were opposed by Beijing's former client, the Khmer Rouge.)

APPENDIX: FORCES OF THE PLA[70]

China's armed forces include the PLA, the reserves/militia, and the People's Armed Police (PAP). The PLA includes the Army, Navy, Air Force, and the Second Artillery Corps.

A. GENERAL ORGANIZATION OF THE PLA

Three departments -- General Logistics Department, General Political Department, and General Staff Department -- provide operational leadership to the PLA. The Commission for Science, Technology and Industry for National Defense supervises weapons research and coordinates the military with the civilian economic sector. The PAP is under the Ministry of Public Security. China's reserves and militia are controlled by the PLA at the military district level only.

The Chinese military is organized into seven military regions (MRs), each capable of an entire spectrum of missions. MRs can be combined into a front command to conduct campaigns.

Regional forces are organized into four categories of units with specific missions. The PLA group army is the highest level tactical organization. Garrison district commands were keys in the "People's War" concept, but now are being eliminated or placed in reserve, due to lack of external threat.

China has determined that its current forces are inadequate for the projected localized conflicts of the near future. To adapt to new threats, rapid reaction units are being organized and trailed. Examples include the 38th Army near Beijing. The PLA is concentrating its limited resources on modernizing and equipping rapid reaction forces, and its other premier units.

The remainder of the PLA is being reorganized. Primary efforts include improving training techniques and standardization, along with coordinating operations between the various service branches.

B. PLA GROUND FORCES (ARMY)

China' army is the world's largest, and is composed primarily of light and motorized infantry. The ground force is organized into 24 group armies, composed of 72 infantry, 12 tank, 2 mechanized, and 7 artillery divisions.

China's ground forces are adequate for defense, but lack power projection abilities, due to reliance on obsolete technology. The PLA's primary objective remains to modernize its forces.

The PLA's main force deploys many obsolete but serviceable weapons such as the Type 59 tank (Soviet T-54). More modern equipment is being produced, but much of the output is destined for external sale. Only a limited number of

[70]For background, see among others the article by Gregory Man in "China: A Nation in Transition," Washington, *Congressional Quarterly*, 1995. Specific figures on Chinese forces were made available at the U.S. congressional hearings on China cited in footnote 2.

new tanks (200-300) are deployed within the PLA. Prototype tanks have been under development for more than fifteen years, but the Chinese lack the funds to produce them in the necessary numbers.

Chinese towed artillery and multiple rocket launchers have strength in numbers and boast of ammunition enhancements. However self propelled systems continue to face difficulties in modernizing. The PLA's towed artillery is among the best in the world, and has been helped by the acquisition of counter battery radars from the West.

Air defense artillery (ADA) gun systems remain the backbone of PLA ADA units. Three surface-to-air missile systems have been deployed in limited numbers to tactical units, but most are 1960's and 1970's vintage.

The PLA's aviation corps is a mix of Soviet and Western systems. The most significant problems for PLA army aviation is maintaining the operational readiness and capability of its systems as preventive maintenance is not widely practiced.

For the remainder of the 1990's, the PLA will have very limited power-projection capabilities. Away from China's rail lines and airfields, the PLA would revert to an infantry force. While extremely tough individually, these forces lack adequate logistical, transport, air defense, communications, armor and air support to fight a modern battle. Development of rapid reaction forces in each group army, enhanced training, and the eventual fielding of modern weaponry will result in limited Chinese ground force projection capabilities in the next decade.

C. NAVAL FORCES

The PLA Navy (PLA-N) ranks as the third-largest in the world, roughly equivalent in size to the Russian Pacific Fleet. Headquartered in Beijing, it consists of three fleet commands: the North Sea Fleet, based at Qingdao, the East Sea Fleet in Shanghai, and the South Sea Fleet in Zhanjing. the majority of China's ships are patrol and coastal combatants effective for coastal defense only.

The PLA-N has only fifty-six principal combatants. Luda destroyers and Jianghu frigates, while good, older designed hulls, have significant problems with onboard weapons, equipment, and power plants. Key deficiencies and areas of development include air defense and electronic warfare. The PLA-N's success in deploying the Luhu destroyer and the Jiangwei frigate will be essential to China's hopes of future naval power projection.

The Chinese submarine force, like its surface brethren, is large in number, but composed of mostly obsolete vessels. China has one operational Xia class submarine and one converted Golf class test bed submarine equipped to launch the JL-1 missile. The principal submarine is the late 1950's Romeo class diesel. Most subs are fitted with dated sensors and weapons. As a partial replacement for the Romeos, the PLA-N has been negotiating with Russia to purchase a small number of Kilo-class submarines that would greatly advance China's submarine capabilities.

For amphibious operations the Navy has the organic sealift capability for one infantry division with tanks for a thirty day deployment. This could provide enough force for a South China Sea/Spratly Islands operation, but nothing larger. Civilian ships could be employed in nontactical situations.

PLA-N aviation lacks the refueling capability needed to provide air support beyond the range of land based planes, and planes are limited to daytime operation. However, a new fighter-bomber, the FB-7, with more operational capability, is being deployed.

R and D ventures consist primarily of developing defensive measures, and are seeking outside assistance.

The PLA-N remains operationally a coastal defense force, but now has the ability to conduct viable operations against Vietnamese held islands in the South China Sea. For the remainder of the 1990's Chinese missions will be limited by defensive and replenishment inadequacies. The Navy has only one 18 ship task force capable of remaining at sea for any sustained period of time. It will continue to strive towards acquiring blue water Navy status, including the possible future acquisition of an aircraft carrier, but that time, at the moment, seems a long way off.

D. AIR FORCE

The PLA Air Force has the world's largest collection of 1950's technology Soviet Aircraft. The Air Force's primary mission is to defend Chinese airspace. Although its large number of aircraft is impressive, the Air Force's lack of modern capabilities make it the weakest part of the PLA force structure.

The PLA-AF's capabilities continue to be seriously hindered by obsolete airframes and powerplants. China's 2,700 F-6 fighters are based on 1950's Soviet models. A possible replacement will have only 1970's technology. China has some modern fighters, but in greatly insufficient numbers.

The most significant acquisition by the PLA-AF has been the purchase and delivery of twenty six Su-27/Flanker long range fighters from Russia. Chinese pilots and support personnel have trained in Russia and are completing advanced training in central China. These state-of-the-art, fourth generation, aircraft will provide a leap in aircraft technology from the second generation F-7's.

China's bomber force is dependent on the 1960's B-6/Badger, which is unlikely to survive in hostile airspace.

The Air Force has serious technological deficiencies. Some progress has been made in aircraft design with Western assistance. The Chinese aircraft industry is turning increasingly to Russian technology sources in order to update its avionics program. The expanding defense relationship between the PLA and Russia's aircraft industry may lead to more sales of modern Russian fighters and equipment.

E. Nuclear Forces

China is the world's fourth largest nuclear power, possessing a small but credible nuclear deterrent force. The nuclear forces are operated by the 100,000 member Strategic Missile Force or Second Artillery, which is controlled by the Military Commission. China's nuclear forces are meant to deter both nuclear and conventional attack. Chinese leaders have pledged never to be the first to use nuclear weapons, but they have accompanied this pledge with a promise of a certain nuclear counterattack if attacked. The PRC maintains its nuclear retaliatory capability by dispersing and concealing its nuclear forces in difficult terrain, improving the mobility of its systems and hardening its missile silos.

Beijing's current missile force consists of more than 100 mobile CSS-2 intermediate range ballistic missiles, a few transportable CSS-3 limited range ICMBs, and as many as twelve silo based CSS-4 ICMBs which can strike targets throughout the U.S., Russia, and Europe. The Second Artillery also has on hand an aging stockpile of less than 100 nuclear bombs. China possesses one Xia class nuclear powered submarine with 12 tubes for the JL-1 Submarine Launched ballistic Missile (SLBM). China has developed the M-9 and M-11 short range ballistic missiles for the international arms market and for deployment in a tactical nuclear mode to PLA field artillery units. For the future, China is developing solid propellant medium range missiles to provide more mobile and reliable systems with faster launch times.

F. Paramilitary Operations

1. Reserves

The National Defense Reserve Force was first noted under the 1985 Central Document No. 22. In theory, these reserve units are integrated into the orders of battle of group armies and other active force units as augmenting or rounding out units. Roughly 80 percent of the forty reserve divisions identified thus far are infantry. Most reserve divisions have been formed in the three military regions adjacent to the Sino-Russian border.

Since 1989, the PLA has established a viable foundation combining its militia and reserve forces. A sizable reserve force composed of such specialized elements as antiaircraft and artillery is being assembled. The tactical and operational abilities of the reserves are being enhanced.

The reserve force has increased China's military capability only modestly, but is better organized and trained than the militia, thus increasing the PRC's wartime capability.

2. Militia and People's Armed Police Force

The PLA militia consists of approximately 4 million armed and 6 million general or ordinary militia. The militia receives sporadic military training and serve as reserves in wartime.

The People's Armed Police was formed in 1983, when the PLA transferred its internal security and border defense units to the Ministry of Public Security. The PAP is responsible for controlling internal security issues, such as Tiananmen. In wartime the PAP perform border defense and support functions. The PAP has about 700,000 personnel.

U.S. TRADE AND MARKET ACCESS PROBLEMS WITH ASIA: AN OVERVIEW

Dick K. Nanto

U.S. MERCHANDISE TRADE WITH ASIA[1]

The United States trades more with the countries of East and Southeast Asia than with NAFTA (Canada and Mexico) or the European Union. East and Southeast Asia are the destination for 21 percent of U.S. exports and 32 percent of U.S. imports.

[1]Prepared by Dick K. Nanto, Specialist in Industry and Trade, Economics Division.

TABLE 1. U.S. Trade with East Asia, APEC, NAFTA, and the World, 1994

Country/Group	U.S. Exports to ($ Million)	U.S. Imports from ($ Million)	Merchandise Trade Balance ($ Million)	Deficit as % of Total Deficit
Japan	53,481	119,149	-6,558	43.4%
South Korea	18,028	19,658	-1,630	1.1%
China/Hong Kong	20,732	48,479	-27,747	18.3%
Taiwan	17,078	26,711	-9,633	6.4%
Total Chinese Economic Area	37,810	75,190	-37,380	24.7%
Total East Asia	109,319	213,997	-104,678	69.1%
Brunei	376	46	330	NA
Indonesia	2,811	6,523	-3,712	2.5%
Malaysia	6,955	13,977	-7,012	4.6%
Singapore	13,022	15,360	-2,338	1.5%
Thailand	4,861	10,307	-5,446	3.6%
Philippines	3,888	5,720	-1,832	1.2%
Vietnam	172	50	122	NA
ASEAN	32,095	51,983	-19,888	13.1%
Total East Asia and ASEAN	141,414	265,980	-124,566	82.3%
Australia	9,781	3,200	6,581	NA
New Zealand	1,508	1,421	87	NA
Chile	2,776	1,822	954	NA
Papua New Guinea	65	108	-43	0.0%
Total APEC	320,639	450,971	-130,332	86.1%
Total NAFTA	165,095	178,440	-13,345	8.8%
Total European Union	102,818	110,875	-8,057	5.3%
Total World	512,416	663,830	-151,414	100.0%

Note: ASEAN includes Brunei, Indonesia, Malaysia, Philippines, Singapore, Thailand, and Vietnam.

Chinese Economic Area = China, Hong Kong, and Taiwan.

NAFTA - Canada, Mexico, United States.

APEC (Asia Pacific Economic Cooperation) = United States, Canada, Mexico, Chile, Japan, South Korea, China, Taiwan, Hong Kong, Australia, New Zealand, and Papua New Guinea.

Source: Data from U. S. Department of Commerce.

APEC and Free Trade in the Asia Pacific[2]

The Asia Pacific Cooperation forum (APEC) is a council of eighteen nations/states bordering on the Pacific Ocean. It includes the United States, Canada, Mexico, Japan, China, Taiwan, Hong Kong, South Korea, ASEAN (Indonesia, Malaysia, Singapore, Thailand, The Philippines, and Brunei, but not Vietnam), Australia, New Zealand, Chile, and Papua New Guinea. This Asia Pacific region contains nearly half the earth's population and more than half the world's production.

In November 1994, President Clinton and the leaders of APEC met in Bogor, Indonesia, and signed a declaration setting a goal to establish free and open trade in the Asia Pacific. Concrete details on this free trade area are yet to be worked out, but the goal is for the industrialized economies (U.S., Japan, Canada, Singapore, Australia, New Zealand, and possibly others) in APEC to achieve free and open trade and investment by the year 2010 and for the rest of the members to do so by the year 2020.[3]

On November 16-19, 1995, the APEC will hold a Leaders' Summit and Ministerial meeting in Osaka, Japan. (Taiwan's President has been barred from attending because of objections from China.) In Osaka, the leaders of APEC are expected to sign an Action Agenda that will lay out general principles for liberalization and facilitation to reach the free trade goal as well as to provide specific items on economic and technical cooperation. The general principles are to lay the basis for individual APEC members to devise their national Action Plans to be submitted to APEC in 1996. Thee plans are to meet the Bogor goal of free trade and investment by 2010 or 2020.

Since Japan is hosting the 1995 APEC meetings, it holds the Chair and responsibility to insure that the APEC process continues. Japan, however, has taken this opportunity to lead a group (including South Korea and China) of countries that have been resisting the principle of comprehensiveness (free trade should apply to all products). They hope to gain some flexibility in liberalizing their agricultural sectors, particularly rice This problem will be addressed by the APEC ministers and leaders in Osaka. The Osaka meetings also will likely result in a proposal for an APEC dispute settlement mechanism and for accelerated implementation of the Uruguay Round tariff reductions.

The APEC declarations, heretofore, have been nonbinding. As the countries submit their Action Plans that will lead to free trade and investment, however, some believe that members will have to officially ratify the plans. If this is the case, for the United States, it may be considered under fast-track authority for approval of trade agreements.

---

[2]Prepared by Dick K. Nanto, Specialist in Industry and Trade, Economics Division.

[3]The extra ten years were allowed the developing nations primarily at the insistence of China, South Korea, and Malaysia. Trade liberalization in APEC is to be on a reciprocal basis to prevent "free riders."

The political question of whether the public would support a free trade area encompassing all key North American and Asian Pacific economies, however, is yet to be answered. In the United States, for example, considering the acrimonious debate over NAFTA, how would the American people respond to a free trade area that included Japan, China, and South Korea?

U.S. exporters have much to gain from the lowering of trade barriers in Asia. The U.S. market is relatively more open than most major markets in Asia. For example, import duties on automobiles in Southeast Asia range between 30 and 60 percent compared to 2.5 percent in the United states. The Asian APEC nations also are some of the fastest growing in the world. They represent multibillion dollar markets for U.S. exporters.

APEC symbolizes post-Cold War relationships in which trade and investment have become an important pillar in the foundation underlying world peace and security. Trade often has become a catalyst for change in countries with authoritarian governments or isolated markets. APEC promotes cooperation and trade among the nations of the Pacific Basin, encourages open trading systems, keeps the United States engaged in the region, and provides the Asia Pacific with a counterweight to the European Union. In response to APEC, the European Union has floated the idea of a trans-Atlantic free-trade agreement.

APEC began as an Australian initiative in 1989. It was a consultative forum at the ministerial level, but in 1993, President Clinton raised its profile by adding a leader's summit. APEC has a small headquarters in Singapore and includes the following working groups: trade and investment data, trade promotion, industrial science and technology, human resources development, regional energy cooperation, marine resource conservation, telecommunications, transportation, tourism, and fisheries.

TRADE RELATIONS WITH JAPAN[4]

The United States and Japan are closely tied economically. Japan ranks second only to Canada as the largest U.S. export market. Japan is the leading market for U.S. agricultural exports, such as corn and meat; for U.S. crude materials such as wood; and for U.S.-produced aircraft. Japan is also the second largest supplier of U.S. imports, including cars, consumer electronics, telecommunications equipment, and computers. The United States ranks as Japan's number one export market and import supplier.

For many years the relationship has been clouded by a persistent, large U.S. trade deficit with Japan. Table 2 below shows that U.S. trade deficits with Japan hit $57 billion in 1987. They declined from 1987 to 1990 as the effects of dollar depreciation took hold. During that period, U.S. exports to Japan soared while U.S. imports from Japan stagnated or grew modestly.

[4] Prepared by William H. Cooper, Specialist in International Trade and Finance, Economics Division.

The trade deficit grew to $65.7 billion in 1994, as the United States experienced economic recovery and growth while Japan remained in recession. In the long run, many economists expect the deficit to shrink once again as Japan emerges from its recession and the effects of a stronger yen in terms of the dollar take hold.

TABLE 2. U.S. Merchandise Trade with Japan, 1987-1995
($ billions)

Year	Exports	Imports	Balances
1987	27.8	84.6	-56.8
1988	37.4	89.8	-52.4
1989	44.5	93.5	-49.0
1990	48.6	89.7	-41.1
1991	48.1	92.3	-44.2
1992	47.8	97.2	-49.4
1993	47.9	107.3	-59.3
1994	53.5	119.1	-65.7
1994 (Jan-Aug)	35.1	77.0	-41.9
1995 (Jan-Aug)	41.8	84.4	-42.6

Source: U.S. Department of Commerce, Bureau of the Census, Trade Net Data Retrieval System. Exports are total exports valued on a f.a.s. basis. Imports are general imports values on a customs basis.

Japan's global current account (merchandise trade, plus services and unilateral transfers) surplus is the largest in the world. Many policymakers have viewed it as an indicator of Japan's protected market and an imbalance in Japanese economic policies that have emphasized savings over consumption. In 1992, Japan's current account surplus was 3.2 percent of its gross domestic product. U.S. officials have argued that a level below 2 percent was more in line with historical trends and would be less disruptive to other economies. They have called on Japan to introduce fiscal policies to stimulate economic growth and reduce this surplus. In 1993, the surplus dropped to about 3.1 percent of GDP and to 2.8 percent in 1994.

U.S. trade policy toward Japan has focused primarily on the problems of access to its markets for American exports. U.S. companies and policymakers have cited a range of barriers, such as import quotas, tariffs, customs procedures, technical specifications, government regulations, and business practices.

The U.S. Government has negotiated with Japan under various formats. These include the Reagan Administration's Market-Oriented Sector-Specific (MOSS) talks, the Bush Administration's Structural Impediments Initiative (SII), and the Clinton Administration's U.S.-Japan Framework for a New Economic Partnership (Framework Talks). All of these efforts have had the same underlying purpose: to open Japan's relatively closed economy to imports. Since even the Japanese agree that the U.S. market is more open than theirs, from the standpoint of fairness and reciprocity, the U.S. position is that Japan must change its policies, practices, and regulations without reciprocal concessions on the part of the United States, although the United States has agreed to take macroeconomic measures to bring more balance into its external trade and capital flows.

The Framework Talks

At the initiative of the Clinton Administration with the eventual support of the Japanese government, on July 10, 1993, U.S. and Japanese negotiators completed the "The United States-Japan Framework for a New Economic Partnership." The Framework is an arrangement for trade negotiations that lays out a "set of rules" under which the talks are to be conducted.

The centerpiece of the Framework is a set of five "baskets" or categories of current and prospective issues in U.S.-Japanese relations: (1) **government procurement**--to expand Japanese government procurement of foreign goods and services, especially computers, supercomputers, satellites, medical technology, and telecommunications equipment; (2) **regulatory reform and competitiveness**--reform of Japanese laws, regulations, and guidance, that have impeded imports of foreign goods and services, including financial services and insurance; (3) trade in **other major sectors**, including autos and auto parts and flat glass; (4) **economic harmonization**--issues affecting foreign direct investment in Japan and the United States, intellectual property rights protection, access to technology, and relationships between buyers and suppliers (for example, the *keiretsu*); and (5) **implementation of exiting agreements and measures**.

Within the Framework, the United States and Japan agreed that the issues would be addressed within specific time frames and that "objective criteria," both qualitative and quantitative indicators, would be used to gauge compliance with agreements. Furthermore, the President and the Prime Minister agreed to meet twice a year to review and announce results obtained under the Framework.

Under the Framework, Japan agreed to take the necessary measures to achieve "a highly significant decrease" in global imports in the "medium term." The United States agreed to take measures towards "substantially reducing" its Federal budget deficit, promoting domestic saving, and strengthening its international competitiveness. The Framework also commits to two countries to work jointly on global issues -- environmental protection, technology development, human resources development, population growth control, and AIDS abatement.

With the use of objective criteria to gauge compliance, the new Framework shifted the focus of U.S.-Japanese trade negotiations away from "process" (changing the rules of trade, such as lowering trade barriers) to "results" (actual sales or market share). The Framework, however, did not define the concept of "objective criteria," and that concept proved to be the most contentious point in almost all of the negotiations that followed.

MARKET ACCESS[5]

The Japanese government has removed many formal barriers to imports of goods and services. Import licenses, still technically required for all goods, are granted on a *pro forma* basis, with limited exceptions (fish, leather goods and some agricultural products). Japan's average industrial tariff rate (about two percent) is one of the lowest in the world, and Japan has agreed to further tariff reductions in the Uruguay Round. The Uruguay Round Agreement will reduce but not eliminate trade barriers in agriculture, manufactured goods, and services.

Traditional trade policy measures, however, are not the greatest obstacles to penetrating Japanese markets. Instead of tariffs and official discrimination against imports, U.S. exporters must deal with numerous factors that raise costs and inhibit access in areas ranging from glass to auto parts. These obstacles include archaic and multi-tiered distribution systems, "keiretsu" (networks between manufacturers and distributors linked by long-time business relationships and often by cross-holding of shares) relationships, excessive government regulation and the use of administrative guidance, public procurement practices, and the high cost of land (which inhibits new market entrants).

Under the Framework Talks, the dispute over access for foreign automobiles and parts has been the most contentious. Although the two nations did reach an agreement on June 28, 1995, it came just hours before a U.S. deadline after which the Clinton Administration was prepared to impose 100 percent tariffs on Japanese-made luxury cars. The dispute illustrates the difficulty of trade negotiations with Japan. Japan imposes no import duties on cars, but the United States claimed that Japanese repair procedures, standards, inspection system, car dealer networks, and model approval mechanism were keeping foreign card and parts from gaining market share in an auto market nearly half as large as that in the United States.

The auto and parts agreement requires the Japanese government to take certain measures such as increasing its enforcement of antitrust laws and changing government regulations on repair and inspection facilities. Two sticking points in the negotiations centered on what objective criteria would be used to measure progress and whether Japanese auto manufacturers would continue to announce their plans to purchase foreign parts in their assembly operations. The Japanese Government claimed that such plans would become numerical targets that it

---

[5] Material in this section, except for the discussion of automobiles and parts, is from: U.S. Department of State. *Economic Policy and Trade Practices: Japan*. August 1, 1995.

could not enforce and which might invite adverse action from the United States if they were not achieved.

On January 10, 1995, the two governments announced a comprehensive financial services agreement that should further open Japan's financial markets to foreign competition. The agreement ensures the U.S. financial institutions have the opportunity to compete more effectively in the Japanese financial market.

In December 1994, the United States and Japan finalized an agreement under the Framework to open Japan's flat glass sector to foreign suppliers. In October 1994, the two countries signed market-opening agreements in insurance and government procurement of medical technology and telecommunications goods and services (including procurement by Japan's massive phone company, Nippon Telegraph and Telephone Corporation). Other agreements in 1994 included improving access to Japan's cellular telephone market, eliminating barriers to imports of apples, and streamlining and improving intellectual property procedures.

In the last few years, Japan also agreed to relax rules on value-added telecommunications services, to strengthen copyright protection for U.S. music recordings, and to resolve a dispute involving amorphous metals, for which market entry has been facilitated. The United States continues to closely monitor U.S.-Japan agreements including those in the areas of commercial satellites, government procurement of supercomputers, semiconductors, construction, wood products, paper, medical products and pharmaceuticals, and computer procurement.

The ability of foreign architectural and construction firms to access Japan's public works market continues to be closely scrutinized by the U.S. government. For many years, Japan has engaged in exclusionary practices which have prevented foreign firms from competing successfully on contracts for major Japanese construction projects. To remedy this situation, the U.S. government negotiated the 1988 Major Projects arrangements (revised in 1991) which gave foreign firms improved access to thirty-four major construction projects. Despite these agreements, U.S. architectural, engineering, and construction firms continued to face difficulties in Japan. As a result, Japan was designated under Title VII of the 1988 Omnibus Trade and Competitiveness Act for discriminatory procurement practices. Following months of intensive negotiations with the United States, in January 1994 Japan adopted a new Action Plan to overhaul its public works procurement system. The Action Plan replaces the designated bidding system (under which only specified companies could offer bids) with an open and competitive system, allows foreign firms' international experiences to be considered when determining a firm's qualifications, and applies to all procurement above a certain threshold, not just the thirty-four major projects.

Although the Japanese government has simplified, harmonized and, in some cases, eliminated restrictive product standards to follow international practices in a number of areas, many problems remain. The 1985-1987 Market-Oriented

Sector Selective (MOSS) Talks resolved many standards problems and set in motion a continuing dialogue through MOSS follow-up meetings of experts.

OPENNESS TO FOREIGN INVESTMENT

Foreign investment into Japan in most sectors is now subject to only *ex post* notification to the Ministry of Finance (MOF). Prior to the SII talks, all foreign investors were required to notify the MOF of their intent to invest 30 days before any investment occurred. Japan still requires prior approval in certain sectors: air and maritime transport, space development, atomic energy, oil and gas production and distribution, agriculture, fisheries, forestry, leather and leather products manufacturing, and tobacco manufacturing.

Foreign investment in the banking and securities industries is subject to a reciprocity requirement. Japan accords foreign investors national treatment after entry, with the Organization for Economic Cooperation and Development (OECD) notified of limited exceptions. The Japanese government does not employ local equity requirements, export performance requirements or local content requirements. The Japanese government has not forced foreign individuals or companies to divest themselves of investments. Japanese law allows foreign landholding, and foreign investors may repatriate capital and profits readily.

TABLE 3. Top Ten U.S. Exports to Japan, 1990 and 1994
(Thousands of dollars)

Commodity	1990	1994
Total all commodities	48,584,647	53,480,756
77--Electrical machry, apparatus & appliances, n.e.s.	2,391,161	3,960,124
75--Office machs and automatic data processing machs	3,679,170	3,789,259
79--Transport equipment, n.e.s.	3,688,392	3,499,704
24--Cork and wood	2,690,506	2,967,626
78--Road vehicles (inc air-cushion vehicles)	1,580,588	2,851,803
89--Miscellaneous manufactured articles, nes	3,448,468	2,679,487
04--Cereals and cereal preparations	2,423,400	2,464,856
87--Professional scient & control inst & apparatus nes	1,615,272	2,228,209
01--Meat and meat preparations	1,567,401	2,210,094
03--Fish (except marine mammal) crustaceans, etc. preps	1,798,697	1,886,375

Source: Compiled from official statistics of the U.S. Department of Commerce.
Top 10 commodities (SITC revision 3) sorted by Total exports, f.a.s. value in 1994

At the same time, inward foreign direct investment in Japan is much lower than that in its major G-7 trading partners. There are a number of factors underlying the low level of inward investment, including the legacy of many years of active Japanese government discouragement of foreign investment. A major problem today, however, is the high cost of doing business in Japan, particularly for new market entrants, that may make the rate of return on investments lower than other alternatives. In addition, foreign acquisition of existing Japanese companies is difficult, due in part to crossholding of shares among allied companies, leading to the limited availability of publicly traded common stock. This practice complicates efforts of foreign firms to acquire exiting distribution/service networks through mergers and acquisitions. The Japanese government has taken some initial steps to provide incentives to foreign investors. This issue is under discussion in Foreign Direct Investment sub-basket of the Framework.

TABLE 4. Top Ten U.S. Imports from Japan, 1990 and 1994
(Thousands of dollars)

Commodity	1990	1994
Total all commodities	90,433,130	119,149,366
78--Road vehicles (inc air-cushion vehicles)	28,114,272	33,931,117
75--Office machs and automatic data processing machs	11,005,826	18,056,961
77--Electrical machry, apparatus & appliances, n.e.s.	8,902,723	15,530,523
76--Telecommun & sound record & reproduce app & equip.	9,389,731	9,178,690
71--Power generating machinery and equipment	3,289,723	5,641,593
74--General industrial machry & equipmt, n.e.s. & pts.	3,860,658	5,154,781
72--Machinery specialized for particular industries	3,335,865	4,592,271
89--Miscellaneous manufactured articles, ne	4,627,930	4,096,364
88--Photo appt, equip & optical goods nes; watch & clk	2,693,021	3,655,157
87--Professional scient & control inst & apparatus nes	1,641,188	2,390,838

Source: Compiled from official statistics of the U.S. Department of Commerce.
Top 10 commodities (SITC revision 3) sorted by Total exports, f.a.s. value in 1994

THE CHINESE ECONOMIC AREA (CEA)

The Chinese Economic Area, which includes China, Hong Kong, and Taiwan, is the largest of what the Department of Commerce calls the "Big Emerging Markets" of the world. The CEA is the seventh largest economic entity in the world (if the European Union is not counted as one economy), with a combined GNP of $809.8 billion for 1993, and it constitutes the third largest trading partner for the United States -- the fourth largest export market and third largest supplier.

The CEA holds large combined foreign exchange reserves and has the largest number and total dollar value of planned infrastructure projects (energy, transportation, telecommunications, and environment) in the world (more than $500 billion on infrastructure related equipment, technologies, and expertise during the next six years).

TRADE WITH CHINA[6]

U.S.-china trade has risen rapidly since 1980, when most-favored-nation (MFN) status was mutually granted. Total trade (exports plus imports) between the two nations rose from $4.8 billion in 1980 to $48.1 billion in 1994. China is now the 6th largest U.S. trading partner. Over the past few years, the U.S. trade deficit with China has grown sharply, due largely to a surge in U.S. imports of Chinese goods relative to U.S. exports to China (see table 5). As a result, the U.S. trade deficit with China has been rising at a faster rate than with any other major U.S. trading partner. In 1984, the United States had a $61 million trade deficit with China. In just 10 years, the U.S. trade deficit with China surged to $29.5 billion, making China the second largest deficit trading partner of the United States behind Japan (see figure 1). U.S. trade data for the first five months of 1995 indicate that the U.S. trade deficit in 1995 could rise to about $37 billion.

TABLE 5. U.S. Merchandise Trade with China: 1984-1995*
($ Millions)

Year	U.S. Exports	U.S. Imports	U.S. Trade Balance
1984	$3,004	$3,065	-$61
1985	3,852	3,862	-10
1986	3,105	4,771	-1,666
1987	3,488	6,293	-2,805
1988	5,033	8,512	-3,479
1989	5,807	11,989	-6,181
1990	4,807	15,224	-10,417
1991	6,278	18,976	-12,698
1992	7,418	25,727	-18,309
1993	8,767	31,535	-22,768
1994	9,287	38,781	-29,494
1995 Estimate*	10,481	46,919	-36,438

*Data for 1995 estimated based on U.S.-China trade data for January-August 1995.

Source: U.S. Department of Commerce

U.S. EXPORTS TO CHINA

U.S. exports to China in 1994 totaled $9.3 billion, accounting for 1.8 percent of total U.S. exports to the world, and making China the 14th largest market for

[6] Prepared by Wayne M. Morrison, Analyst in International Trade and Finance, Economics Division.

U.S. exports. At present, Chin is a relatively small market for U.S. exports. For example, U.S. exports to China are smaller than those to such Asian countries as Hong Kong, Singapore, South Korea, and Taiwan. However, China is becoming one of the fastest growing markets for U.S. exports. U.S. exports to China between 1990 and 1994 grew by 93.2 percent. U.S. exports to China in 1995 are projected to rise by about 15 percent over the previous year.

FIGURE 2. U.S. Merchandise Trade with China, 1984–1994

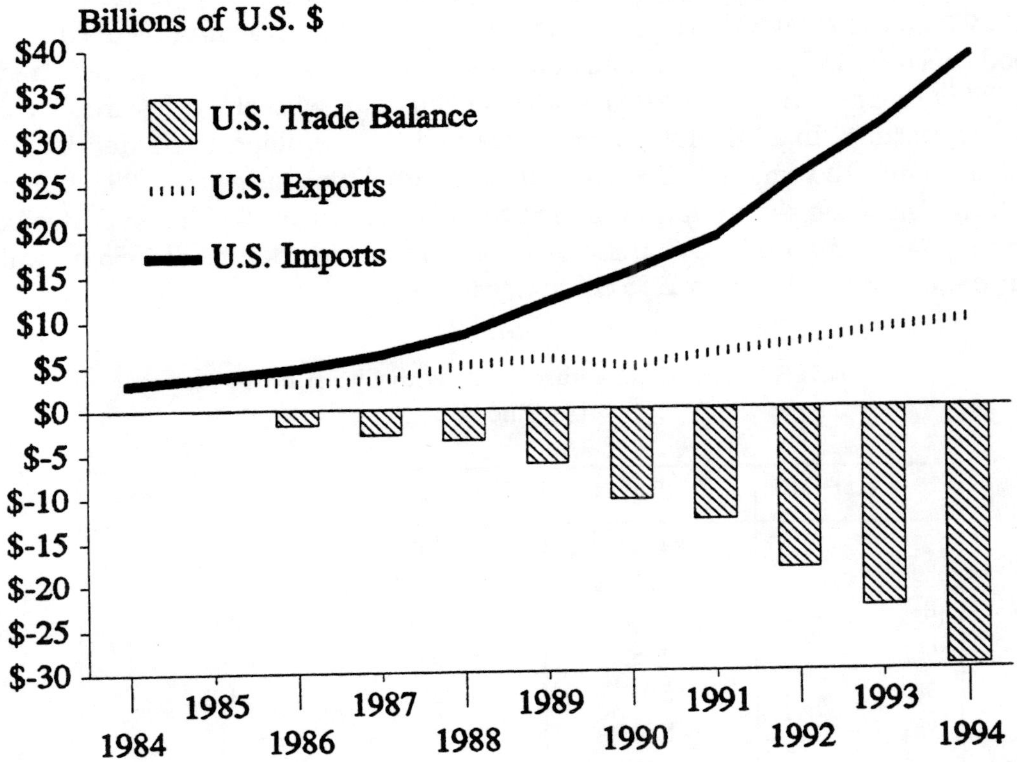

The top five U.S. exports to China in 1994 were (1) transport equipment (mainly aircraft and parts), (2) fertilizers, (3) textile fibers, (4) specialized machinery, and (5) telecommunication and sound equipment. Together, these five commodities accounted for over half of total U.S. exports to China. Aircraft and parts were by far the largest U.S. export to China in 1994, accounting for 20.9% of total U.S. exports.

U.S. Imports From China

China is a relatively large source of many U.S. imports. In 1994, imports from China accounted for 5.8% of total U.S. imports, making China the fourth largest supplier of U.S. imports. The level of U.S. imports from china nearly doubled between 1991 and 1994; U.S. imports from China are projected to rise by over 25 percent in 1995.

The top five U.S. imports from China in 1994 were (1) miscellaneous manufactured articles (such as toys, games, etc.); 2) clothing and apparel; (3) footwear; (4) telecommunications equipment, sound recording, and reproducing equipment (such as telephone answering machines, radios, tape recorders and players, televisions, VCRs, etc.); and (5) electrical machinery. Together, imports of these five commodities accounted for over two-thirds of total U.S. imports from China. U.S. imports from China in 1994 rose by $7.2 billion (or 23.0%) over the previous year. Imports of miscellaneous manufactured articles, clothing, and footwear accounted for a substantial share of this increase.

The surge in U.S. imports of Chinese products over the past few years can be largely explained by two factors. First, China's production of low-cost, labor-intensive products (such as consumer goods) has increased sharply in recent years (due to China's comparative advantage in such sectors); U.S. demand for such products has steadily increased as well. Secondly, Hong Kong and Taiwan have shifted production of a wide variety of labor-intensive products (such as shoes, toys, and electronic products) into China to take advantage of China's relatively low-cost labor supply. As a result, many of the products which used to be produced in Taiwan and Hong Kong (a large share of which were exported to the United States) are now being produced for export by Hong Kong and Taiwanese firms in China.

CHINA -- MARKET ACCESS AND TRADE ISSUES[7]

Of the three CEA markets, tariffs are highest in China. Customs regulations are not uniformly applied in China, making exporting there unpredictable at times. U.S. exporters may also face arbitrary determinations of value by customs officials, and there are frequent reports of being charged different rates for the same product. Most special economic zones, open cities and foreign trade zones offer preferential duty reductions or exemptions.

Import taxes, in the form of a value-added tax (VAT) and other taxes, are levied in addition to tariffs on items entering China, adding to costs for exporters. China collects a value-added tax, generally equal to 17 percent, on imported items. Certain luxury items are also subject to a consumption tax ranging from 3 to 45 percent.

China uses non-tariff barriers extensively to regulate trade investment. This is a subject of intense negotiation in discussions regarding accession to the GATT/WTO. While numerous barriers have been removed since 1992, China continues to administer a complex system of individual quotas, import licensing requirements and a tendering system applied to both quota and non-quota

[7]Prepared by Wayne M. Morrison, Analyst in International Trade and Finance, Economics Division.

commodities, among others. China currently retains non-tariff measures (quotas, licenses or tenders) for 784 tariff line items. The absence of transparency is a further barrier to U.S. exports.

Many trade analysts have attributed the growing U.S.-China trade deficit to China's restrictive trade practices. Other trade issues of concern to the United States have included China's violation of U.S. intellectual property rights (IPR), transshipments of textiles to the United States in violation of U.S. textile quotas, and China's alleged use of forced labor for products exported to the United States. Over the past few years, the United States and China have reached agreements on many of these issues:

- On April 26, 1991, the United States Trade Representative (USTR) designated China under Special 201 for failing to provide adequate protection for U.S. intellectual property rights. A memorandum of understanding (MOU) was reached on January 16, 1992. However, on June 30, 1994, the USTR again designated China under Special 301 for failing to enforce its IPR laws and for restricting market access of intellectual property-related products. On February 4, 1995, the USTR announced that sanctions would be imposed against China by February 26, 1995, unless a new agreement was reached. A preliminary agreement was subsequently reached on February 26, 1995, which pledges China to significantly improve its IPR enforcement regime and market access for U.S. products.
- On October 10, 1991, the USTR initiated a Section 301 investigation of four major Chinese trade barriers, including import prohibitions and quotas, restrictive import license requirements, restrictive standards and certification requirements for imports, and lack of transparency of Chinese trade laws. On October 10, 1992, the United States and China reached an MOU agreement on market access. China agreed to reduce several major trade barriers over the next five years. China suspended its implementation of the MOU agreement in January 1995 after it was unable to obtain membership into the World Trade Organization (WTO) by the end of 1994. However, in March 1995, China agreed to resume its implementation of the MOU, after the United States reportedly assured China that it supported China's accession to the WTO and would be flexible on China's accession terms.
- On August 7, 1992, the United States and China signed a MOU to ensure that products made by forced labor in China are not exported to the United States. On March 14, 1994, China agreed to take additional steps to provide access to suspected forced labor camps for U.S. inspectors.
- On January 17, 1994, the United States and China reached an agreement on U.S. import quotas of Chinese textile and apparel products which would limit the growth in China's quota levels and establish mechanisms to deal with Chinese transshipments.

China's increasing trade surplus with the United States and alleged unfair trade practices have become a focal point in the annual congressional debate over China's MFN status. Over the past few years, several Members of Congress have attempted to pass legislation terminating or conditioning China's MFN status. On June 2, 1995, President Clinton announced his decision to renew China's MFN status for an additional year. On July 20, 1995, the House tabled legislation (H.J. Res. 96) which would have terminated China's MFN status and instead passed H.R. 2212 which urges the President to press China on human rights, trade, and arms exports, and to report its efforts to the Congress every six months.

While the United States and China have reached agreement on several trade areas, it is likely that tensions will persist in the near future. The trade issues likely to cause the most conflict include:

- **The U.S.-China trade imbalance**. The U.S. trade deficit with China continues to grow sharply and could increase to $37 billion in 1995.
- **Market access**. The United States continues to press China to improve market access for U.S. goods and services by seeking to get China to implement fully the October 1992 MOU on market access. The UTR has noted on several occasions that China has not fully implemented the agreement. For example, China continues to maintain restrictive phytosanitary inspection requirements on agricultural imports. In addition, China has failed to remove all tariff and non-tariff barriers on specific products which were designated under the MOU. Finally, problems remain over the transparency of China's trade laws and regulations. The USTR has warned on several occasions that sanctions could be imposed against China if the agreement is not fully carried out.
- **The World Trade Organization (WTO)**. The United States is holding talks with China over its accession to the WTO. The United States has insisted that China make major reforms to its trade regime before it is allowed to become a member of the WTO, including making its trade regime more transparent, significantly reducing government support of domestic firms, and affording national treatment to foreign firms. Chinese officials have argued that China should be allowed to enter the WTO as a developing country, and thus be afforded a transitional period to implement trade reforms after it becomes a WTO member. Chinese officials have been reluctant to reduce several trade barriers apparently out of fear that such measures could be disruptive to certain Chinese industries. China views the United States as the largest impediment to its becoming a member of the WTO.
- **IPR enforcement.** Disputes will likely arise in the future over China's implementation of the February 1995 IPR agreement as well as the pace and

degree of market-opening measures. The Chinese government has pledged to conduct extensive raids over the next several months against firms producing pirated materials and to strengthen its IPR enforcement regime. In addition, China pledged to establish a coordinated IPR enforcement approach at all levels of government to stop piracy. However, in the past, the central government has often had difficulty getting provincial and local governments to enforce laws and regulations issued by the central government.

- **Political issues**. U.S.-China economic relations could be affected by policy issues related to Chinese actions on human rights, weapons proliferation, and Taiwan. China might respond to U.S. policies by limiting trade or restricting U.S. investment.

Openness to Foreign Investment

China's legal and regulatory system is characterized by a general lack of transparency and inconsistent enforcement, creating uncertainly for foreign investors. In China, there are over 150 major laws and regulations which apply to foreign trade and investment, and many of these laws and regulations are fraught with ambiguities. Foreign firms usually do not receive national treatment.

China's leadership is attempting to reform the legal system to rationalize the various sets of regulations governing commercial activity, and in the past few years, it has made a number of reforms to improve its trade regime -- mainly in high-priority sectors of the economy where foreign investment is considered to be critical (e.g., energy, telecommunications, transport, etc.). Even if a project meets one or more of the government's investment screening requirements, it may still be rejected if it is determined that the contract is unfair, that the technology is available elsewhere in China, or that China already has sufficient production capacity of the particular product.

Several types of barriers to foreign investment exist in China:

- The government usually requires firms to set up production facilities in order to sell in the domestic market.
- Pressure is put on foreign firms to establish export-oriented operations.
- Usually, foreign firms are required to operate as joint ventures with Chinese firms. These ventures are highly regulated.
- The government often requires foreign firms to hire a certain number of Chinese citizens. Restrictions also exist on the distribution of products produced.

While China's investment laws and regulations do not require technology transfers, they strongly encourage it, and foreign investors are likely to encounter pressure to agree to such transfers.

TABLE 6. Top Ten U.S. Exports to China, 1990 and 1994
(Thousands of dollars)

Commodity	1990	1994
Total all commodities	4,807,332	9,286,759
79--Transport equipment, n.e.s.	755,387	1,937,661
56--Fertilizers (except crude of group 272)	543,854	944,121
26--Textile fibers & their wastes (exc wool tops etc)	385,856	761,005
72--Machinery specialized for particular industries	323,128	675,985
76--Telecommun & sound record & reproduce app & equip.	81,177	572,007
74--General industrial machry & equipmt, n.e.s. & pts.	179,043	520,111
77--Electrical machry, apparatus & appliances, n.e.s.	136,826	298,202
78--Road vehicles (inc air-cushion vehicles)	50,371	297,228
73--Metalworking machinery	75,020	295,928
87--Professional scient & control inst & apparatus nes	191,028	287,748

Source: Compiled from official statistics of the U.S. Department of Commerce.
Top 10 commodities (SITC revision 3) sorted by Total exports, f.a.s. value in 1994

TABLE 7. Top Ten U.S. Imports from China, 1990 and 1994
(Thousands of dollars)

Commodity	1990	1994
Total all commodities	15,223,887	38,781,143
89--Miscellaneous manufactured articles, nes	3,243,283	8,689,946
84--Articles of apparel and clothing accessories	3,469,429	6,310,738
85--Footwear	1,477,406	5,259,130
76--Telecommun & sound record & reproduce app & equip.	1,163,234	3,798,523
77--Electrical machry, apparatus & appliances, n.e.s.	656,938	2,274,560
75--Office machs and automatic data processing machs	117,652	1,618,088
83--Travel goods, handbags and similar containers	696,117	1,560,660
65--Textile yarn, fabrics, made-up articles, n.e.s.	657,868	1,044,730
69--Manufactures of metals, n.e.s.	381,419	979,147
82--Furniture & pts; bedding, mattresses, etc.	144,581	751,906

Source: Compiled from official statistics of the U.S. Department of Commerce.
Top 10 commodities (SITC revision 3) sorted by Total exports, f.a.s. value in 1994

HONG KONG -- MARKET ACCESS[8]

As one of the most open markets in the world and one of the most successful export processing zones, Hong Kong has a minimum of market access barriers and imposes no incentives or disincentives on trace and foreign investment.

TARIFFS AND IMPORT BARRIERS

Tariffs are applied to only five items in Hong Kong. Customs regulations are uniformly applied in Hong Kong. Domestic consumption taxes (referred to as duties in Hong Kong) are imposed on five items, including tobacco, soft drinks, alcoholic beverages, methyl alcohol and some fuels. These taxes are levied equally on local manufactures and imports.

For Hong Kong, import taxes are negligible. Hong Kong importers are assessed a trade declaration charge of 0.035 percent (35 cents for every $1,000).

Non-tariff barriers to trade are minimal in Hong Kong. However, one barrier for new-to-market firms is the oligopolistic nature of some Hong Kong business. The absence in Hong Kong of any antitrust law or enforcement agency has enabled large conglomerates to dominate certain sectors, and many companies attempting to enter the market for the first time may find channels blocked by existing relationships. The government's policy, however, is to discourage unfair trade practices and is committed to improving competition.

OPENNESS TO FOREIGN INVESTMENT

In Hong Kong, the market dries investment. Hong Kong imposes no scheme of incentives or disincentives on foreign investors, and there is no government policy designed to channel their efforts into specified projects or sectors.

INTELLECTUAL PROPERTY RIGHTS

Hong Kong's market is mostly free of infringing products, its law are solid, and enforcement, for the most part, is effective. While Hong Kong vigorously enforces its intellectual property rights laws, companies selling in this market must be vigilant. Theft of intellectual property still occurs, often in the process of transshipping bonded goods. The best protection for an American company is to have a strong local presence. Good products are most likely to be copies when a firm is not participating in the market.

[8]Prepared by the U.S. Department of Commerce.

TABLE 8. Top Ten U.S. Exports to Hong Kong, 1990 and 1994
(Thousands of dollars)

Commodity	1990	1994
Total all commodities	6,840,413	11,445,345
77--Electrical machry, apparatus & appliances, n.e.s.	1,081,988	2,010,748
75--Office machs and automatic data processing machs	385,445	857,305
97--Gold, nonmonetary (excluding ores & concentrates)	382,036	825,524
66--Nonmetallic mineral manufactures, n.e.s.	412,300	571,786
76--Telecommun & sound record & reproduce app & equip.	172,099	529,309
89--Miscellaneous manufactured articles, nes	343,908	519,650
78--Road vehicles (inc air-cushion vehicles)	23,225	457,330
57--Plastics in primary form	360,415	447,589
79--Transport equipment, n.e.s.	575,556	384,132
01--Meat and meat preparations	111,598	326,555

Source: Compiled from official statistics of the U.S. Department of Commerce.
Top 10 commodities (SITC revision 3) sorted by Total exports, f.a.s. value in 1994.

TABLE 9. Top Ten U.S. Imports from Hong Kong, 1990 and 1994
(Thousands of dollars)

Commodity	1990	1994
Total all commodities	9,488,032	9,697,693
84--Articles of apparel and clothing accessories	3,990,823	4,405,455
77--Electrical machry, apparatus & appliances, n.e.s.	796,361	1,146,424
89--Miscellaneous manufactured articles, nes	1,290,834	1,044,285
75--Office machs and automatic data processing machs	812,163	792,497
88--Photo appt. equip & optical goods nes; watch & clk	546,276	452,778
93--Special transactions & commod not classif by kind	225,266	360,308
76--Telecommun & sound record & reproduce app & equip.	495,624	276,618
65--Textile yarn, fabrics, made-up articles, n.e.s.	203,430	203,967
66--Nonmetallic mineral manufactures, n.e.s	161,098	146,875
69--Manufactures of metals, n.e.s.	164,806	128,342

Source: Compiled from official statistics of the U.S. Department of Commerce.
Top 10 commodities (SITC revision 3) sorted by General imports, Customs value in 1994.

TAIWAN - MARKET ACCESS[9]

Access to Taiwan's market has improved as a result of gradual market liberalization and, more recently, its drive to become a regional operations center and member of the GATT/WTO. Reduced tariffs, a revised customs law and reductions in the number of products requiring import licenses have improved the export climate. Taiwan offers a number of investment incentives to encourage investment, and screening it, as a rule, routing and non-discriminatory.

TARIFFS AND IMPORT BARRIERS

Tariffs are lower in Taiwan than in China. No systemic problems in customs regulations exist for exporters to Taiwan. In the past five years, Taiwan has made significant progress in reducing tariffs on non-agricultural products of interest to U.S. exporters. Taiwan has also agreed to abide by the GATT customs valuable code.

Like China, Taiwan also levies import taxes, in the form of a value-added tax (VAT) and other taxes. Taiwan importers must also pay a 5 percent value-added tax and a 0.5 percent harbor construction fee. A commodity tax must also be paid if an imported product falls into one of eight commodity categories. Rates range from 2 to 60 percent and on a few important products, most notably autos, Taiwan imposes commodity taxes at higher rates for certain types of products not produced locally.

Taiwan uses non-tariff barriers selectively and with less frequency than China. Taiwan's use of non-tariff barriers is, like China's, a subject of intense negotiation in discussions regarding accession to the GATT/WTO. Taiwan continues to maintain an import licensing system, but the number of items requiring import licenses is being gradually reduced.

GOVERNMENT PROCUREMENT PRACTICES

As in China, U.S. firms have been hindered in the bidding on major projects in Taiwan by non-transparent bidding procedures. In negotiations regarding its GATT/WTO accession, Taiwan has committed to adhering to international practices with regard to government procurement. U.S. firms have a well-established record of success in winning tenders which are administered by Taiwan's Central Trust of China (CTC). However, the bulk of Taiwan authority purchases are administered by the purchasing entities themselves, not the CTC. These tenders may be restricted to firms with a local presence, and it can be difficult for outsiders to obtain advance information on them.

In the course of negotiations on its GATT/WTO accession, Taiwan has committed to joining the new WTO Government Procurement Agreement

[9]Prepared by the U.S. Department of Commerce.

(GPA) scheduled for implementation in January 1996. This should serve to open significant public procurement opportunities to the U.S. and suppliers from other signatories (including Japan, Canada and the EU).

Openness to Foreign Investment

Taiwan has established three export processing zones in order to encourage investment and to expand the export of products and services. All products imported by enterprises located in these zones for their own use are exempt from customs duties. As a rule, Taiwan relies on investment incentives to encourage the development of particular industries.

Although applications for investment approvals are screened in both China and Taiwan, U.S. investors will find that this process is much more predictably non-discriminatory in Taiwan. In Taiwan, applications for investment approval are screened to determine whether the investment project is subject to foreign investment decisions.

Meanwhile, restrictions on investment in Taiwan are relatively transparent, and investors can easily determine those sectors which are closed to foreign investment or where it is limited. The "negative list," adopted in July 1990, clearly specifies industries closed to foreign investment, including 54 prohibited industries and 55 industries where foreign ownership is still limited.

Intellectual Property Rights

Taiwan is in the process of developing a comprehensive legal system and is improving protection of intellectual property as well as enforcement. A series of

TABLE 10. Top Ten U.S. Exports to Taiwan, 1990 and 1994
(Thousands of dollars)

Commodity	1990	1994
Total all commodities	11,482,403	17,077,650
77--Electrical machry, apparatus & appliances, n.e.s.	1,439,705	2,782,599
79--Transport equipment, n.e.s.	429,960	1,528,890
51--Organic chemicals	867,387	1,321,497
78--Road vehicles (inc air-cushion vehicles)	847,209	1,294,478
89--Miscellaneous manufactured articles, nes	441,882	770,590
04--Cereals and cereal preparations	659,306	733,200
76--Telecommun & sound record & reproduce app & equip.	577,382	562,716
75--Office machs and automatic data processing machs	470,011	540,680
74--General industrial machry & equipmt, n.e.s. & pts.	493,871	536,146
87--Professional scient & control inst & apparatus nes	275,833	461,864

Source: Compiled from official statistics of the U.S. Department of Commerce.
Top 10 commodities (SITC revision 3) sorted by Total exports, f.a.s. value in 1994.

important laws have been passed since 1992, including revised copyright, patent and trademark laws, a U.S.-Taiwan bilateral copyright agreement and a cable television law. Together with new legislation under consideration to protect integrated circuit designs and trade secrets, these laws give Taiwan an IPR legal structure largely consistent with international practices.

Although improved enforcement efforts have reduced the incidence of copyright violations, inconsistencies in the trademark and patent area highlight the need for more standardized examination and registration procedures. The U.S. government recently moved Taiwan from "priority watch" to the "watch list" under the Special 301 provision of the 1988 Trade Act.

TABLE 11. Top Ten U.S. Imports from Taiwan, 1990 and 1994
(Thousands of dollars)

Commodity	1990	1994
Total all commodities	22,666,672	26,710,738
75--Office machs and automatic data processing machs	3,092,090	6,094,951
77--Electrical machry, apparatus & appliances, n.e.s.	2,193,614	3,929,556
89--Miscellaneous manufactured articles, nes	2,991,571	2,619,298
84--Articles of apparel and clothing accessories	2,488,525	2,266,560
69--Manufactures of metals, n.e.s.	1,560,698	2,047,931
76--Telecommun & sound record & reproduce app & equip.	1,450,785	1,214,440
82--Furniture & pts; bedding, mattresses, etc	1,008,630	1,181,573
74--General industrial machry & equipmt, n.e.s. & pts	846,191	1,080,166
78--Road vehicles (inc air-cushion	870,794	910,783
65--Textile yarn, fabrics, made-up articles, n.e.s.	444,070	577,488

Source: Compiled from official statistics of the U.S. Department of Commerce.
Top 10 commodities (SITC revision 3) sorted by Genera imports, Customs value in 1994.

SOUTH KOREA - MARKET ACCESS[10]

South Korea is one of the most difficult markets in Asia to invest in and export to. Its policies remain structured primarily to encourage technology transfer and optimize the use of imports for export industries while discouraging "unnecessary" imports. The problems in the business climate are both systemic and sector-specific. Much of the government-to-government dialogue between the U.S. and South Korea has been aimed at removing these barriers.

[10]Prepared by the U.S. Department of Commerce.

Tariffs and Import Barriers

Most South Korean tariffs are assessed on an ad valorem basis. Specific rates apply to a few items, and both ad valorem and specific rates apply on a few others. The dutiable value of imported goods is the normal c.i.f. price at the time of import declaration. Tariffs are payable in won before the goods are permitted to clear customs. In January 1994, South Korea completed a five-year tariff reduction plan which reduced the average tariff rate on imports to 7.9 percent. Duties remain very high (25 percent on average), however, on a large number of high-value agricultural and fisheries products. Pursuant to its Uruguay Round commitments, on January 1, 1995, South Korea lowered duties on some agricultural products and eliminated duties on products in the paper, toys, steel, semiconductor and pharmaceutical sectors. South Korea also bound 90 percent of its tariff lines, which will curtail its ability to raise duties in the face of import surges of low-value goods (e.g., emergency tariffs). Frequently, over the past few years, the government has invoked provisions of its Customs Law to apply special tariff rates under certain adverse economic conditions.

Government Procurement Practices

The Office of Supply, Republic of Korea (OSROK) supervised procurement by government agencies and most of the state-owned firms in which the government holds a majority share. (Korea Telecom and Korea Electric Power Company are the two largest entities not covered by OSROK procurement). OSROK covers roughly one-half of the total of South Korean government non-defense procurement, with total procurement levels at $816 million in 1993, $883 million in 1994 and $925 million (estimated) in 1995. Government procurement needs are formulated by the ministries and agencies concerned, then screened by the Ministry of Trade and Industry to determine if the needs can be met by local sources. If not, the Ministry of Finance and Economy allocates the necessary foreign exchange. To encourage South Korean firms to develop the needed technologies, OSROK has been releasing three-year forecasts of major requirements in April of each year. The system thus discriminates against all foreign suppliers in cases where goods or services are available domestically.

However, foreign-invested companies manufacturing in South Korea can qualify as domestic sources. For American business to participate effectively in the South Korean government market, it helps to have a local representative.

Openness to Foreign Investment

The South Korean regulatory environment, difficult even for South Korean firms, poses a particular challenge to the foreign investor. Laws and regulations are often framed generally. The meaning of the law in practice thus depends on discretionary interpretations by working-level officials, increasing the opportunities for inconsistent application, discrimination and corruption. Working-level officials often rely on unpublished internal ministerial guidelines and unwritten administrative guidance in interpreting and administering the law.

The reforms that are part of President Kim's five-year economic plan are designed to attract foreign investment and technology. These policy changes, combined with continuing bilateral efforts to improve the business climate for foreign investors, have already eased some of the problems of doing business, but more needs to be done. There is already some positive effect; foreign investment in South Korea is increasing, probably as a result of the government's measures to improve the investment climate.

South Korea fully recognizes rights of private ownership and has a well-developed body of laws governing the establishment of corporate and other business enterprises. Private entities may generally acquire and dispose of interests in business enterprises in South Korea. However, the Securities and Exchange Act provides that no legal person (individual or firm) may own more than 10 percent of a publicly-listed corporation.

Intellectual Property Rights

Intellectual Property Rights (IPR) protection has remained a top issue on the U.S. trade agenda with South Korea for nearly a decade. The U.S. government has frequently received complaints from U.S. firms about infringement of patents, copyrights, trademarks and trade secrets by South Korean firms, covering a wide range of product areas: film, video and sound recordings; compact discs; computer software; textiles; footwear; pharmaceuticals; high technology; and consumer goods. Since April 1992 South Korea has been cited on the priority watch list under the Special 301 provision of U.S. trade law for poor IPR enforcement and delayed improvements to several IPR laws.

In February 1993, the South Korean government began a concerted effort to improve and enforce its IPR laws to satisfy U.S. government and private sector concerns. However, U.S. firms still regularly experience IPR-related difficulties in South Korea. This is because enforcement, while responsible to U.S. complaints, is neither self-initiated nor preventive in nature. South Korea needs to accelerate and expand its efforts to heighten awareness in its business community to international norms and standards for the protection of IPR. Therefore, Commerce says it cannot be emphasized too strongly that all U.S. firms should first register for IPR protection with the appropriate government agency before beginning to do business in South Korea.

Anti-Import Sentiment of South Korean Government and Media

Throughout 1990 and 1991, after the South Korean government had initiated a public campaign to curb excessive consumption and promote austerity, the U.S. government received numerous reports of discriminatory treatment of U.S. consumer product in South Korea. Examples of such activities included: removal of imported products from store shelves, limitations on promotional activities and threats of tax audits of South Korean purchasers of imported automobiles. U.S. firms also reported long delays in customs clearance for imported agricultural and consumer goods, and difficulty in receiving product registrations and approvals.

TABLE 12. Top Ten U.S. Exports to South Korea, 1990 and 1994 (Thousands of dollars)

Commodity	1990	1994
Total all commodities	14,398,720	18,028,362
77--Electrical machry, apparatus & appliances, n.e.s.	1,394,798	2,340,053
79--Transport equipment, n.e.s.	961,527	1,728,716
74--General industrial machry & equipmt, n.e.s. & pts.	704,729	999,271
76--Telecommun & sound record & reproduce app & equip.	306,968	956,315
72--Machinery specialized for particular industries	549,035	798,175
75--Office machs and automatic data processing machs	655,702	777,482
51--Organic chemicals	694,738	745,066
87--Professional scient & control inst & apparatus nes	470,588	722,083
89--Miscellaneous manufactured articles, nes	500,611	678,060
21--Hides, skins and furskins, raw	780,077	632,296

Source: Compiled from official statistics of the U.S. Department of Commerce.

Top 10 commodities (SITC revision 3) sorted by Total exports, f.a.s. value in 1994.

TABLE 13. Top Ten U.S. Imports from South Korea, 1990 and 1994 (Thousands of dollars)

Commodity	1990	1994
Total all commodities	18,493,163	19,657,552
77--Electrical machry, apparatus & appliances, n.e.s.	2,505,983	4,926,817
75--Office machs and automatic data processing machs	1,351,174	2,538,663
84--Articles of apparel and clothing accessories	3,257,142	2,220,790
76--Telecommun & sound record & reproduce app & equip.	1,708,117	1,958,906
78--Road vehicles (inc air-cushion	1,292,626	1,656,160
89--Miscellaneous manufactured articles, nes	1,562,978	1,170,127
85--Footwear	2,573,003	680,536
65--Textile yarn, fabrics, made-up articles, n.e.s.	488,408	608,621
67--Iron and steel	573,993	567,359
69--Manufactures of metals, n.e.s.	568,463	537,627

Source: Compiled from official statistics of the U.S. Department of Commerce.

Top 10 commodities (SITC revision 3) sorted by Genera imports, Customs value in 1994.

In the face of U.S. pressure, the South Korean government publicly announced that the intent of the campaign was not to discriminate against imports and reaffirmed its commitment to further trade liberalization. Subsequently, anti-import activities waned and, since 1992, have arisen less frequently (usually at year's end in order to improve South Korea's trade balance). They are usually confined to certain regions of the country (undertaken by local governments).

INDONESIA - MARKET ACCESS[11]

TARIFFS AND IMPORT BARRIERS

In 1986, the Indonesian Government began liberalizing its trade policies. Periodic deregulation packages have eliminated or reduced tariffs and non-tariff barriers. Tariffs range from 5 to 200 percent, with the majority falling between 5 and 40 percent. Indonesia's simple average import tariff fell from 37 percent in 1985 to about 20 percent in 1992. The average effective tariff is much lower, however, due to exemptions. Approximately 50 percent of potential duties used to produce exported goods, and imports exempted by the Ministry of Finance. Smuggling and under-invoicing also reduce the effective tariff rate.

Import surcharges, or supplemental import duties, apply to 200 customs tariff lines. The surcharges range from 5 to 100 percent (the highest figure is applied to imports of motor vehicles).

GOVERNMENT PROCUREMENT PRACTICES

Since many of the major companies in Indonesia are state-owned, the government of Indonesia is a major customer for a variety of products and services. These cover the full range of defense materials, items needed for infrastructure projects, research and development programs, and several of the pure industrial needs categorized under "Strategic Industries," which are under national government control. These industries include steel making, ship building, aircraft assembly, some electronics and communications manufacturing.

Generally, government procurement is financed through foreign donors. Each donor in turn imposes its own procurement requirements. The government of Indonesia recently enacted a new procurement law, but "economically weaker" local groups and domestic products continue to be given preferences.

OPENNESS TO FOREIGN INVESTMENT

The Foreign Capital Investment Law of 1967, with later amendments, provides the basic framework for foreign investment. The Capital Investment Coordinating Board (BKPM) plays a key role in promoting foreign investment and ap-

[11] Prepared by the U.S. Department of Commerce.

proving project applications. Investments in the oil and gas, mining, banking and insurance industries are handled by the relevant technical government departments. All other foreign investment must be approved by the BKPM, which also approves domestic investments when the owners seek investment incentives. BKPM aims to function as a one-stop investor service; however, investors also need to work closely with relevant technical government departments and with regional and local authorities.

Since the early 1980s, the government has implemented a series of economic reforms to improve the investment climate and to encourage private sector activity. In June 1994, the government dropped initial equity requirements for most types of foreign investment and sharply reduced divestiture requirements. It has simplified procedures for obtaining foreign investment approvals and offered foreign investors incentives, including duty exemptions on capital equipment. The list of sectors closed to foreign investment is quite short, but the ban on direct foreign involvement in distribution continues to hinder trade, although the government has made some progress. Historically, only 100 percent domestically-owned companies were allowed to participate in trading activities -- defined as the import, export, distribution and sale of imported an domestic goods and services.

INTELLECTUAL PROPERTY RIGHTS

Intellectual property protection has improved significantly with the passage of copyright, patent and trademark legislation. Enforcement, however, still poses

TABLE 14. Top Ten U.S. Exports to Indonesia, 1990 and 1994
(Thousands of dollars)

Commodity	1990	1994
Total all commodities	1,896,735	2,811,002
79--Transport equipment, n.e.s.	380,249	451,241
26--Textile fibers & their wastes (exc wool tops etc)	223,083	274,351
72--Machinery specialized for particular industries	166,265	250,169
51--Organic chemicals	108,232	164,677
71--Power generating machinery and equipment	77,703	153,194
25--Pulp and waste paper	64,533	143,054
74--General industrial machry & equipmt, n.e.s. & pts.	100,062	134,818
77--Electrical machry, apparatus & appliances, n.e.s.	48,530	103,927
57--Plastics in primary forms	86,534	103,555
76--Telecommun & sound record & reproduce app & equip.	39,506	83,208

Source: Compiled from official statistics of the U.S. Department of Commerce.
Top 10 commodities (SITC revision 3) sorted by Total exports, f.a.s. value in 1994.

some problems. Indonesia is a member of the World Intellectual Property Organization and is party to certain sections of the Paris Convention for the Protection of Intellectual Property. Indonesia's first patent law entered into effect on August 1, 1991. The law and its implementing regulations outline patent applications, procedures, application fees, registration of patent consultants and patent announcements.

A new trademark act took effect on April 1, 1993. This act states that trademark rights re determined an a first-to-file basis rather than on a fist-use basis.

TABLE 15. Top Ten U.S. Imports from Indonesia, 1990 and 1994
(Thousands of dollars)

Commodity	1990	1994
Total all commodities	3,343,108	6,523,439
84--Articles of apparel and clothing accessories	635,480	1,127,033
85--Footwear	240,811	884,497
76--Telecommun & sound record & reproduce app & equip.	12,915	710,102
33--Petroleum, petroleum products & related materials	917,222	706,458
23--Crude rubber (including synthetic & reclaimed)	424,317	575,825
63--Cork and wood manufactures other than furniture	362,073	448,493
07--Coffee, tea, cocoa, spices & manufactures thereof	171,255	299,302
89--Miscellaneous manufactured articles, nes	60,602	287,880
82--Furniture & pts; begging, mattresses, etc.	55,676	186,678
03--Fish (except marine mammal) crustaceans, etc. preps	102,765	183,739

Source: Compiled from official statistics of the U.S. Department of Commerce.

Top 10 commodities (SITC revision 3) sorted by Genera imports, Customs value in 1994.

MALAYSIA -- MARKET ACCESS[12]

TARIFFS AND IMPORT BARRIERS

Malaysia has few trade barriers. Import permits are generally not required. Import duties range from zero to 300 percent, but on most goods the duty is 10 percent. Also, Malaysia exacts a 10 percent sales tax on most imports, but imports of products not available locally and used for export production are exempt from both the duty and sales tax. U.S. semiconductor companies operating in Malaysia have benefited from this provision. Licensing requirements cover primarily arms, explosives, motor vehicles, controlled substances, some raw materials and agricultural products. Malaysia has agreed to substantial tariff re-

[12]Prepared by the U.S. Department of Commerce.

ductions on a wide range or products to comply with GATT and World Trade Organization standards.

Malaysia has no foreign exchange restrictions that would impede trade or repatriation of profits. Local agents are required for sales to the government and are "highly recommended" for sales to the private sector.

Government Procurement Practices

Generally, types of tenders are issued by the Malaysian government--local and international. Foreign contractors are not allowed to bid on local tenders, while on international tenders, there are no prohibitions on U.S. contractors to bid, and no licenses are required. Foreign contractors interested in participating in turnkey projects must be prequalified by the Implementation and Coordination Unit (ICU) of the Prime Minister's department before they can tender.

To perform construction in Malaysia, U.S. firms need to have a local representative -- which may be Malaysian or American. If a U.S. company wants to win construction projects, it will need to have a Malaysian partner. In general, local joint venture partners should have at least 30 percent equity in the partnership and play an active role in the implementation of the project.

As with other countries, government officials tend to view contractors more favorably if they use Malaysian products and services to the extent possible.

Openness to Foreign Investment

The Promotion of Investment Act of 1986 and the Industrial Coordination Act of 1974 specify investment guidelines. The Malaysian Industrial Development Authority (MIDA) screens proposals for a manufacturing license to determine whether or not they are consistent with the Industrial Master Plan (IMP) and government social policy. Approval depends on the size of the investment, whether or not it includes local equity participation, the type of financing (both local and offshore) required, the ability of existing and planned infrastructure to support the effort, and the existence of a local or foreign market for the output. MIDA applies the criteria in a non-discriminatory manner, except in rare instances when a local and a foreign firm propose identical projects. One-hundred percent foreign ownership in manufacturing is permitted only in certain instances.

Intellectual Property Rights

Malaysia has one of the region's strongest regimes for protecting intellectual property rights (IPR). In fact, the Business Software Alliance gave Malaysia an aware in 1992 for its vigilance against software piracy.

Most patents registered in Malaysia are good for a relatively short period of 15 years. The duration can be extended under certain circumstances. Processing time for trademark registration may be as long as 18 months. Copyright protection extends to computer software and lasts for life plus 50 years.

TABLE 16. Top Ten U.S. Exports to Malaysia, 1990 and 1994
(Thousands of dollars)

Commodity	1990	1994
Total all commodities	3,424,700	6,964,767
77--Electrical machry, apparatus & appliances, n.e.s.	1,740,319	3,199,621
79--Transport equipment, n.e.s.	427,865	946,343
75--Office machs and automatic data processing machs	139,614	354,230
71--Power generating machinery and equipment	46,759	324,321
72--Machinery specialized for particular industries	141,628	209,044
89--Miscellaneous manufactured articles, nes	32,232	200,931
87--Professional scient & control inst. & apparatus nes	100,999	190,670
74--General industrial machry & equipment, n.e.s. & pts	97,174	171,828
76--Telecommun & sound record & reproduce app & equip.	48k437	163,133
66--Nonmetallic mineral manufactures, n.e.s	12,712	109,730

Source: Compiled from official statistics of the U.S. Department of Commerce.
Top 10 commodities (SITC revision 3) sorted by Total exports, f.a.s. value in 1994.

TABLE 17. Top Ten U.S. Imports from Malaysia, 1990 and 1994
(Thousands of dollars)

Commodity	1990	1994
Total all commodities	5,272,333	13,977,161
76--Telecommun & sound record & reproduce app & equip.	1,229,630	4,006,862
77--Electrical machry, apparatus & appliances, n.e.s	1,767,387	3,979,442
75--Office Machs and Automatic data processing machs.	197,449	2,532,421
84--Articles of apparel and clothing accessories	612,504	1,049,581
89--Miscellaneous manufactured articles, nes	196,949	412,076
82--Furniture & pts; begging, mattresses, etc.	38,065	301,708
88--Photo appt, equip & optical goods nes; watch & clk	45,303	196,317
63--Cork and wood manufactures other than furniture	44,273	156,730
23--Crude rubber (including synthetic & reclaimed)	133,610	145,139
42--Fixed veg, fats & oils crude, refined, fractionate	100,433	126,665

Source: Compiled from official statistics of the U.S. Department of Commerce.
Top 10 commodities (SITC revision 3) sorted by Genera imports, Customs value in 1994.

The Philippines - Market Access[13]

Tariffs and Import Barriers

There are some barriers that make market entry in the Philippines difficult, including quantitative restrictions on more than 100 agricultural and industrial items. Overall tariff rates are still relatively high at about 22 percent, and further reductions are planned. Customs valuations procedures were based on the "home consumption value," (HCV) rather than invoice value until January 1995, which sometimes resulted in arbitrary and unreasonably high valuations of U.S. exports. The Philippines is moving to implement a transaction-based valuation system that will be introduced sometime within the next five years, but potential customs valuations problems remain.

An ongoing tariff reduction, restructuring and simplification program was completed by July 1, 1995, on schedule. It lowers the average nominal tariff to 20 percent, grouped into four tiers of 3, 10, 20 and 30 percent. Discussions are underway in the Philippine government on further tariff reductions to the year 2000.

Government Procurement Practices

The Philippine government is a large, direct importer of many essential products, including road building equipment and military and defense equipment. Government agencies pattern their regulations and procedures after those of the U.S.

Procurement regulations permit a foreign company to bid on government projects only if it maintains a registered branch office or a registered resident agent in the Philippines. The first step in obtaining government business is to be placed on the Bidder's Mailing List of the agency with which the applicant is interested in doing business.

Openness To Foreign Investment

In the investment area, there are continuing restrictions on company and land ownership. The 1991 Foreign Investment Act (FIA) allows foreign equity in Filipino enterprises to exceed 40 percent, provided no investment incentives are sought and provided the company does not engage in an activity which appears on the "negative list." Pending legislation, supported by the government, seeks to abolish this list altogether. In 1994, the law was amended to simplify rules and regulations, permit negotiations on unsolicited proposals (for private sector-initiated projects not necessarily on the government's priority list), and permit projects valued in excess of one billion pesos to apply for government incentives.

[13] Prepared by the U.S. Department of Commerce.

INTELLECTUAL PROPERTY RIGHTS

In recent years, the Philippines has not consistently and effectively protected intellectual property rights, in part as a result of inadequate laws and regulations and insufficient resources for enforcement. The Philippines was moved

TABLE 18. Top Ten U.S. Exports to The Philippines, 1990 and 1994 (Thousands of dollars)

Commodity	1990	1994
Total all commodities	2,471,574	3,888,329
77--Electrical machry, apparatus & appliances, n.e.s.	675,007	1,717,697
04--Cereals and cereal preparations	175,933	283,233
76--Telecommun & sound record & reproduce app & equip.	38,557	189,134
72--Machinery specialized for particular industries	95,420	145,966
71--Power generating machinery and equipment	73,699	145,559
74--General industrial machry & equipment, n.e.s. & pts	94,837	123,318
75--Office machs and automatic data processing machs	63,268	82,350
64--Paper, paperboard and articles thereof	52,700	81,324
89--Miscellaneous manufactured articles, nes	56,350	75,976
87--Professional scient & control inst. & apparatus nes	34,467	69,156

Source: Compiled from official statistics of the U.S. Department of Commerce.

Top 10 commodities (SITC revision 3) sorted by Total exports, f.a.s. value in 1994.

TABLE 19. Top Ten U.S. Imports from The Philippines, 1990 and 1994 (Thousands of dollars)

Commodity	1990	1994
Total all commodities	3,382,598	5,720,275
77--Electrical machry, apparatus & appliances, n.e.s	746,771	1,865,554
84--Articles of apparel and clothing accessories	1,077,084	1,412,079
76--Telecommun & sound record & reproduce app & equip.	185,762	440,280
89--Miscellaneous manufactured articles, nes	245,083	299,746
88--Photo appt, equip & optical goods nes; watch & clk	71,436	245,167
42--Fixed veg, fats & oils crude, refined, fractionate	125,721	185,749
75--Office Machs and Automatic data processing machs.	80,830	151,528
05--Vegetables and fruit	124,385	150,740
82--Furniture & pts; begging, mattresses, etc.	111,387	139,821
03--Fish (except marine mammal) crustaceans, etc. preps	89,453	99,138

Source: Compiled from official statistics of the U.S. Department of Commerce.

Top 10 commodities (SITC revision 3) sorted by Genera imports, Customs value in 1994.

from the U.S. Trade Representative's Special 301 "priority watch list" to the regular "watch list" following an agreement signed in April 1993, in which the government committed itself to significantly strengthen protection of intellectual property rights in the Philippines. The Philippine government is currently considering draft legislation on patents, trademarks and copyrights which it intends to submit to the Philippine Congress in 1995.

SINGAPORE - MARKET ACCESS[14]

TARIFFS AND IMPORT BARRIERS

Singapore imposes very few tariffs on imports; 96 percent of imports enter duty-free. Singapore currently maintains tariffs on less than one percent of its tariff lines (non-petroleum trade) in comparison with the U.S. which has bound 98 percent of its tariff lines. A government tax of 4 percent and a service charge of 10 percent are levied on hotel and restaurant bills. As of April 1, 1994 Singapore implemented a three percent Goods and Services Tax. Essentially a form of value-added tax or VAT, the GST applies to all business of at least S$1 million in goods and services in Singapore; all services received from overseas are also taxable. The tax is anticipated to remain in effect for five years. This tax has significant implications for firms doing or anticipating business in Singapore. Firms will have to adjust their pricing policies to determine the amount of increase in costs to pass on to the customer. Because of the GST levy system, terms of credit in the retail arena will increasingly favor cash over credit.

GOVERNMENT PROCUREMENT PRACTICES

Singapore is noted for its largely transparent procurement practices. With few exceptions, virtually all procurements are accomplished through open international tenders. Almost no complaints are heard from American competitors about procurement processes.

OPENNESS TO FOREIGN INVESTMENT

Singapore's open investment policy overcomes land, resource and labor limitations by selectively encouraging firms that can build up the country's technological base and bring about improvement in the skills of its labor force. The Singapore Economic Development Board acts as the "business architect," identifying sectors with high potential for contributing to the economy, and drafting tax and fiscal incentives to encourage foreign investment in these targeted sectors. The Board also provides a one-stop service for foreign investors, and helps them to avoid the proverbial red tape. Investors are free to purchase material

[14] Prepared by the U.S. Department of Commerce.

from any source and are not limited by access to foreign exchange or required local entity ownership in the investment. Every company, however, must have at least two directors--one of which must reside in Singapore.

Government policies encourage local firms to form strategic partnerships with multinational corporations (MNCs), especially in high technology activities. There are no taxes on capital gains and no restrictions on foreign ownership of businesses. Foreign investors are not required to take on private or official joint ventures or cede management control to local interests. The Economic Development Board assists foreign and locally-owned firms to invest in new technology, automation, training and product development activities though a variety of incentives.

INTELLECTUAL PROPERTY RIGHTS

U.S. companies can be somewhat secure in Singapore's intellectual property rights (IPR) protection and prosecution of violators. Singapore enacted a strict, comprehensive copyright legislation in 1987 and strengthened the Trademark Law in 1991. An even stronger patent protection law went into effect in February 1995.

Singapore recently became a member of the World Intellectual Property Organization (WIPO), but does not subscribe to any international agreement such as the Universal Copyright Convention (UCC) or the Berne Convention.

GOVERNMENT-LINKED CORPORATIONS

A major facet of Singapore's economy of which American suppliers should be aware is that many of the country's top companies are actually government-

TABLE 20. Top Ten U.S. Exports to Singapore, 1990 and 1994
(Thousands of dollars)

Commodity	1990	1994
Total all commodities	8,019,122	13,021,557
77--Electrical machry, apparatus & appliances, n.e.s.	1,635,865	3,385,386
75--Office machs and automatic data processing machs	1,061,115	1,578,484
79--Transport equipment, n.e.s.	716,897	1,539,745
89--Miscellaneous manufactured articles, nes	573,177	778,246
71--Power generating machinery and equipment	444,553	640,457
72--Machinery specialized for particular industries	449,230	518,724
74--General industrial machry & equipment, n.e.s. & pts	342,230	494,964
33--Petroleum, petroleum products & related materials	152,101	479,768
87--Professional scient & control inst. & apparatus nes	278,781	420,198
76--Telecommun & sound record & reproduce app & equip.	212,708	321,416

Source: Compiled from official statistics of the U.S. Department of Commerce.
Top 10 commodities (SITC revision 3) sorted by Total exports, f.a.s. value in 1994.

linked corporations (GLCs) -- state-owned companies. some 44 percent of the economy is accounted for by GLCs including such world-class firms as Singapore Airlines, Singapore Technologies, Chartered Industries, the Keppel Group and the Sembawang Group. GLCs typically operate as if they were purely private companies seeking to maximize profits. Although they will respond to official requests to undertake special projects and tasks, they normally behave as private-sector companies, and they usually have strong financial backing.

TABLE 21. Top Ten U.S. Imports from Singapore, 1990 and 1994
(Thousands of dollars)

Commodity	1990	1994
Total all commodities	9,839,485	15,360,457
75--Office Machs and Automatic data processing machs.	4,354,607	8,674,511
77--Electrical machry, apparatus & appliances, n.e.s	1,513,075	2,496,538
76--Telecommun & sound record & reproduce app & equip.	1,270,894	1,112,851
51--Organic chemicals	305,979	513,913
84--Articles of apparel and clothing accessories	622,843	472,287
93--Special transactions & commod not classif by kind	356,690	357,073
89--Miscellaneous manufactured articles, nes	194,720	277,918
87--Professional scient & control inst & apparatus nes	98,538	275,903
74--General industrial machry & equipmt, n.e.s. & pts.	264,215	254,487
71--Power generating machinery and equipment	98,137	189,801

Source: Compiled from official statistics of the U.S. Department of Commerce.

Top 10 commodities (SITC revision 3) sorted by Genera imports, Customs value in 1994.

Thailand - Market Access[15]

Tariffs and Import Barriers

There are trade barriers to overcome in exporting to Thailand, including high import duties, arbitrary customs valuation, and illegal copying and piracy of copyright, patents and trademarks. High import duties have been a major trade barrier for U.S. exporters, with current duty rates in the 30 to 60 percent range for many products. As part of Thailand's investment promotion strategy, duty exemptions are a routine part of incentives offered to investors, and import duties on raw materials are rebated upon export of finished product. In recent years, the Thai government has taken major steps to reduce and simplify import tariffs to open its market to imports. To comply with GATT standards, Thailand is reducing duties on many manufactured goods.

[15] Prepared by the U.S. Department of Commerce.

GOVERNMENT PROCUREMENT PRACTICES

U.S. exporters have actively pursued government procurement opportunities mostly in the power generation and transmission, petroleum, refining, and petrochemicals, telecommunications, transportation, environment, health care and defense equipment sectors. For U.S. firms, the key to successful bidding on Thai government contracts and supply tenders is to have a reputable local representative with good access to the procuring agency and knowledge of specific requirements and practice. Without the assistance of an effective representative, it is very difficult to sell to the government. Local representatives are an accepted, legitimate part of the bidding process. Agents often alert U.S. firms to attractive tenders and before tenders are issued, they will work to ensure that the principal's product is specified.

The "Prime Minister's Procurement Regulations" govern public sector procurement. The regulations specify non-discriminatory treatment for all potential bidders. The regulations, however, do provide preferential treatment for domestic suppliers, who receive an automatic 15 percent advantage over foreign bidders in initial-round bid evaluation.

OPENNESS TO FOREIGN INVESTMENT

The most serious investment barriers are complicated specifications regulating foreign ownership and control of companies, including several sectors in which foreigners are simply prohibited from participation. The U.S.-Thai Treaty of Amity and Economic Relations allows U.S. citizens and businesses incorporated in the U.S. to engage in business on the same basis as Thais. In return, Thais are extended reciprocal rights to invest in the U.S. Notwithstanding their treaty rights, many American firms choose to form joint ventures with Thai partners and allow them to hold majority shares because of their familiarity with the Thai economy and local regulations. Relations between the U.S. and Thailand are excellent, although trade issues, such as protection of intellectual property rights, dominate the bilateral agenda.

The treaty exempts U.S. businesses operating in Thailand from most foreign exchange restrictions imposed by the Alien Business Decree. In the Uruguay Round of GATT negotiations, Thailand agreed to liberalize its investment regime, granting to all foreigners the same privileges granted to American investors within 10 years.

Thailand restricts American investment only in the fields of communications, transport fiduciary functions, banking, the exploitation of land or other natural resources, and domestic trade in agricultural products. A lack of an agreement between the U.S. and Thailand that eliminates double taxation raises the cost of doing business there.

INTELLECTUAL PROPERTY RIGHTS

Inadequate protection is still a serious issue for U.S. copyright, patent and trademark holders in Thailand. U.S. firms are advised to protect their intellectual property rights by registering their patents and trademarks. Lawyers specialized

TABLE 22. Top Ten U.S. Exports to Thailand, 1990 and 1994
(Thousands of dollars)

Commodity	1990	1994
Total all commodities	2,991479	4, 861,003
77--Electrical machry, apparatus & appliances, n.e.s.	603,577	985,424
74--General industrial machry & equipment, n.e.s. & pts	137,721	366,638
89--Miscellaneous manufactured articles, nes	190,401	360,098
79--Transport equipment, n.e.s.	479,664	318,674
75--Office machs and automatic data processing machs	126,091	294,264
76--Telecommun & sound record & reproduce app & equip.	82,283	235,949
72--Machinery specialized for particular industries	120,116	214,573
51--Organic chemicals	82,490	139,024
87--Professional scient & control inst. & apparatus nes	55,926	130,428
26--Textile fibers & their wastes (exc. wool tops etc)	131,636	122,498

Source: Compiled from official statistics of the U.S. Department of Commerce.
Top 10 commodities (SITC revision 3) sorted by Total exports, f.a.s. value in 1994.

TABLE 23. Top Ten U.S. Imports from Thailand, 1990 and 1994
(Thousands of dollars)

Commodity	1990	1994
Total all commodities	5,293,824	10,307,201
75--Office Machs and Automatic data processing machs.	522,068	1,836,801
03--Fish (except marine mammal) crustaceans, etc. preps	593,186	1,292,489
77--Electrical machry, apparatus & appliances, n.e.s	600,614	1,157,611
89--Miscellaneous manufactured articles, nes	711,622	1,063,022
84--Articles of apparel and clothing accessories	483,085	984,059
76--Telecommun & sound record & reproduce app & equip.	486,259	944,335
85--Footwear	295,477	374,513
66--Nonmetallic mineral manufactures, n.e.s.	228,185	315,721
23--Crude rubber (including synthetic & reclaimed)	82,548	201,639
05--Vegetables and fruit	161,906	198,168

Source: Compiled from official statistics of the U.S. Department of Commerce.
Top 10 commodities (SITC revision 3) sorted by Genera imports, Customs value in 1994.

in intellectual property protection can be used to take legal action to suppress piracy, although this can be a lengthy process. The Thai government is taking legislative and administrative steps to improve enforcement of the exiting copyright law and to pass a stronger copyright law, while the country remains on the U.S. Trade Representative's Special 301 "priority watch list."

VIETNAM - MARKET ACCESS[16]

Market access is problematic, as the appropriate rules and regulations are in a constant state of flux. The universe of licensed importers is small but growing, however, foreign exchange availability may impinge on purchases. Customs can be high, but this is less of a concern than simply finding a legal importer who has an exchange allocation. Domestic distribution is largely restricted to locally-owned companies.

Likely customers include large numbers of recently formed state-owned companies that are still figuring out what a free market is all about. There are growing numbers, too, of private firms, some of which show remarkable entrepreneurship.

TABLE 24. Top Ten U.S. Exports to Vietnam, 1990 and 1994
(Thousands of dollars)

Commodity	1990	1994
Total all commodities	7,445	172,223
79--Transport equipment, n.e.s.	0	72,334
26--Textile fibers & their wastes (exc. wool tops etc)	0	16,982
56--Fertilizers (except crude of group 272)	0	16,533
76--Telecommun & sound record & reproduce app & equip.	289	10,648
72--Machinery specialized for particular industries	12	7,626
78--Road vehicles (inc air-cushion vehicles)	0	5,931
71--Power generating machinery and equipment	23	4,426
93--Special transactions & commod not classif by kind	6,845	4,162
74--General industrial machry & equipment, n.e.s. & pts	0	3,674
87--Professional scient & control inst. & apparatus nes	19	3,155

Source: Compiled from official statistics of the U.S. Department of Commerce.

Top 10 commodities (SITC revision 3) sorted by Total exports, f.a.s. value in 1994.

On July 11, 1995, President Clinton announced the establishment of full diplomatic relations between the United States and Vietnam. This will pave the way for the implementation of many U.S. Government services, trade promotion and

[16] Prepared by the U.S. Department of Commerce.

financing programs normally available to the business community such as Ex-im bank, OPIC, and TDA but currently not available to companies exploring the Vietnam market. Banking, shipping, insurance and other trade facilitating services for direct U.S.- Vietnam trade are still in the early stages of development. With normalization, the US&FCS will soon establish a post in Hanoi to serve American companies, which are facing fierce competition for market share. However, the very positive reception American companies and business people currently enjoy in Vietnam should go a long way toward building strong business ties.

Commercial relations are expected to improve further when new opportunities become available as the economy develops. Existing Vietnamese preference for U.S. goods and services, if coupled with competitive pricing and attractive financing terms, is expected to be sufficient to overcome disadvantages which the United States faces as a latecomer to this important emerging market.

TABLE 25. Top Ten U.S. Imports from Vietnam, 1990 and 1994
(Thousands of dollars)

Commodity	1990	1994
Total all commodities	0	50,450
07--Coffee, tea, cocoa, spices, & manufactures thereof	0	31,193
03--Fish (excpt marine mammal) crustaceans, etc. preps	0	5,830
04--Cereals and cereal preparations	0	4,554
84--Articles of apparel and clothing accessories	0	2,538
42--Fixed beg. fats & oils crude, refined, fractionate	0	1,408
32--Coal, coke and briquettes	0	1,105
83--Travel goods, handbags and similar containers	0	487
05--Vegetables and fruit	0	486
93--Special transactions & commod not classif. by kind	0	329
98--Estimate of low valued import transactions	0	317

Source: Compiled from official statistics of the U.S. Department of Commerce.
Top 10 commodities (SITC revision 3) sorted by Genera imports, Customs value in 1994.

Subject Index

J

K

L

M

N

O

P

R

S

T